Benjamin Franklin

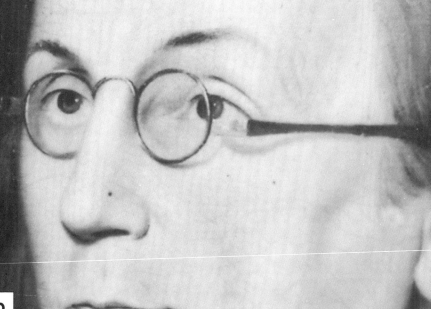

Benjamin Franklin

ROBERT R. POTTER

Silver Burdett Press, Inc.

CONSULTANTS:

Robert M. Goldberg
Consultant to the Social Studies Department
(and former Department Chair)
Oceanside Middle School
Oceanside, New York

Arnold Markoe
Professor
Brooklyn College
City University of New York

PHOTOGRAPH ACKNOWLEDGMENTS:
Culver Pictures, Inc.: pp. 10, 17; Courtesy of The Franklin Institute, Philadelphia, PA:
pp. 95, 98, 105; The Historical Society of Pennsylvania: pp. ii, 130; New York Public
Library Picture Collection: pp. 9, 77, 102, 131; North Wind Picture Archives: 5, 37,
61, 71, 74, 84, 124, 126.

SERIES DESIGN:
R STUDIO T Raúl Rodríguez and Rebecca Tachna

PHOTO RESEARCH:
Omni-Photo Communications, Inc.

Published by Silver Burdett Press, Inc., a division of Simon & Schuster, Inc.,
Englewood Cliffs, NJ 07632.

Library of Congress Cataloging-in-Publication Data
Potter, Robert R. (Robert Russell)
Benjamin Franklin / Robert R. Potter.
p. cm.—(Pioneers in change)
Includes bibliographical references and index.
Summary: Follows the life of the American renaissance man who achieved notable
success as printer, stateman, inventor, author, and reformer.
1. Franklin, Benjamin, 1706–1790—Juvenile literature.
2. Statesmen—United States—Biography—Juvenile literature.
3. Printers—United States—Biography—Juvenile literature.
4. Scientists—United States—Biography—Juvenile literature.
[1. Franklin, Benjamin, 1708–1790. 2. Statesmen. 3. Printers. 4. Scientists.]
I. Title.
E302.6.F8P67   1991
973.3'092—dc20
[B]   90-26029
[92]   CIP
                                                               AC
Manufactured in the United States of America.
ISBN 0-382-24173-8   [lib. bdg.]
10 9 8 7 6 5 4 3 2 1
ISBN 0-382-24178-9 [pbk.]
10 9 8 7 6 5 4 3 2 1

CONTENTS

1

A Birth in Boston

The name Benjamin Franklin has had a kind of electric sparkle to it for well over two hundred years. To this day, Franklin remains America's leading pioneer in change. Among other things:

- It was Benjamin Franklin who flew the famous kite in the thunderstorm and later became the best-known scientist in colonial America.
- It was Benjamin Franklin who first suggested a union of the thirteen original colonies: "We must all hang together, or assuredly we shall all hang separately."
- It was Benjamin Franklin who invented the lightning rod, bifocal glasses, and the Franklin stove.
- It was Benjamin Franklin who charmed the world with wit and wisdom in *The Way to Wealth* and other works.
- It was Benjamin Franklin who helped write and then signed both the Declaration of Independence and the Constitution of the United States.

In a more basic sense, however, it was young Ben Franklin who set out to create the happy, successful, and useful man he later became. In a way, Franklin's most famous invention was himself. His well-known *Autobiography* sets forth his rules for living the good life. These rules have helped millions of readers face the future with calm eyes, a wise smile, and an easy laugh.

The child who became Benjamin Franklin was born in Boston, Massachusetts, on January 17, 1706. That was so far back in time as to make Boston almost a different place from the city we call Boston today. Although its eleven thousand people made it the largest city in colonial America, Boston was, by our standards, small, gray, drab, and dirty. Its claim to fame was a fine harbor, the largest port in the colonies. As many as thirty ships could tie up at the long Boston wharves at the same time. The low hills ringing the harbor bristled with small wooden houses. Some streets were cobbled, or paved with stone. Other streets were more like scars running every which way in the sandy soil.

Most of the people on those streets were of English descent. Among them were well-dressed merchants and government officials. There were also ragged young people who had been talked into coming to the New World— or even kidnapped—then sold as indentured servants. (An indentured servant agreed to serve a master for a period of years, usually in return for the cost of passage, then room and board.) On the streets as well were some black slaves and a few American Indian servants. And animals were everywhere. Pigs rooted around in the garbage that collected in the center of the V-shaped streets. Chickens squawked and scurried at the sudden rumble of horse-drawn carts. Here and there a youth could be seen leading a cow or other animal out to the community pasture that is still called Boston Common.

Beyond the Common, for a few miles, lay the farms and timberland that supported the city. And beyond these lay the edge of what appeared to European settlers as a nearly untracked wilderness. The few British settlements in western Massachusetts lived in constant danger of what even Boston sometimes feared: the French and their Indian allies. At the time, the New World was one of the prizes sought in an ongoing struggle between two Old World powers, England and France. Just two years before Franklin's birth, in fact, the little Massachusetts town of Deerfield had been the scene of a terrible massacre. Early one February morning, French soldiers and Abenaki Indian warriors had surprised the sleeping settlement, killing about fifty men, women, and children before carrying over a hundred people off as captives.

Human enemies were not, however, the main danger faced by the Bostonians of the time. Diseases were the enemies most feared. Modern medicine had hardly begun; most doctors were self-appointed bumblers. During Franklin's youth, for instance, a smallpox epidemic felled half of Boston and killed many. Even in normal times, death was very much a part of life. Work was hard and diets poor. People shivered through the long winters and spent the summers swatting at flies. Infants were especially at risk. It was not uncommon for a man to outlive half his children. Women married early and might expect to bear ten children, or sometimes twenty. Many men outlived a first wife, worn out by years of childbearing and toil, then took a second.

Ben Franklin's family fits this pattern exactly. His father, Josiah Franklin, was born in the little English town of Ecton. As a young man Josiah was apprenticed—or sent for labor and training—to a dyer of cloth. He took up the trade. Josiah married a woman named Anne, who in rapid order bore three children. In 1683, seeking religious freedom and a better life, Josiah Franklin loaded his family on a ship for the long, hard sail to Massachusetts. (The east-to-west voyage then took two months or more.) The years after their arrival produced two more healthy children. But the next baby, born in 1688, lived only five days. And the year after that, Anne Franklin herself failed to survive the birth of her seventh child, who also died.

The death of a wife and two babies in a two-year period was a tragedy, but it was not too unusual in Josiah Franklin's time. Life was for the lucky living; it had to go on. A few months later, at age thirty-one, Josiah took a new wife. His five living children again had a mother. Twenty-two-year-old Abiah was from an "old" Massachusetts family, the Folgers. (It will prove significant that Abiah's own mother had been an indentured servant who married her master when she came of age.) Over the years Abiah Franklin was to give birth to ten children of her own. The eighth of these children was named Benjamin.

Thus Benjamin Franklin was his father's fifteenth child. He was the last boy, and the last child but two. In later years, when Franklin had a chance to do research at Ecton, he discovered that he was the last son of the last son for at least five generations.

In his *Autobiography,* Franklin says strangely little about his mother. He simply indicates that she was the loving, near-perfect mother of a loving son. About his father, however, Ben says a great deal. On arriving in the New World, Josiah Franklin found there was no work for a dyer. He was forced to learn a new trade, making candles and soap. By

Benjamin Franklin was born in 1706 in this house in Boston, Massachusetts.

the time baby Benjamin arrived, Josiah had opened his own shop in a house on Milk Street. The family business took up most of the first floor, on the street side. Josiah, Abiah, and the children lived behind the shop, on the second floor, and in the low attic.

Josiah Franklin was a serious, intelligent, hardworking man. For his time, he was also an educated man. He could read and write. Not only that, he could read and write well. He had a small library of books on religion, and he insisted that the family spend a good part of Sunday at the Old South Church, right across the street. Benjamin later wrote that his father

> could draw prettily, was skilled a little in music, and had a clear pleasing voice, so that when he played psalm tunes on his violin and sung withal, as he sometimes did in an evening after the business of the day was over, it was extremely agreeable to hear. He had a mechanical genius too, and, on occasion, was very handy in the use of other tradesmen's tools; but his great excellence lay in a sound understanding and solid judgment.

A sound understanding and solid judgment. Here Franklin seems to praise in his father what he most admires in himself. Although it was necessary for Josiah Franklin to keep "close to his trade," he was "frequently visited by leading people" for advice. Other people came to him to settle arguments. At family meals, he guided the talk in a way "which might tend to improve the minds of his children." At this he was successful with at least one child. Ben learned not to care much about "what kind of food was set before me." In other words, for this rare boy, food for the mind was more important than food for the body.

Certainly, young Ben Franklin was a bright child. ("I do not remember when I could not read," he later said.) Although his older brothers had been put to different trades at an early age, Ben was sent to the best private school in

Boston. His parents and their friends were determined that he must have a real education. Josiah had a fanciful idea that his tenth son should be his tithe—or tenth part—to the church, and become a minister. So at age eight, Ben entered what later became the famous Boston Latin School. Since he could already read well, he was put in the second class. He soon advanced to the top.

Then the ever-practical nature of Josiah Franklin took over. He began to fear the expenses that would go on year after year if Ben were to go through the grades and then on to Harvard College. Josiah told his friends that, after all, a lot of educated people really didn't do too well in life. Perhaps a good trade was a safer bet than all the education in the world. The result was that the next year Ben was sent to a less costly "school for writing and arithmetic." "I acquired fair writing pretty soon," he commented later, "but I failed in the arithmetic, and made no progress in it."

There followed another blow. Ben's second year in school was to be his last. His older brother John had been apprenticed to their father in the candle-and-soap business. Now John was old enough to go out on his own. He wanted to get married, go off to another colony, and open his own shop. This meant that Josiah Franklin would need a new worker. How could he get the most help for the least money? Easy. By taking his youngest son out of school. "At ten years old," Benjamin wrote later, "I was taken home to assist my father in his business."

He hated the work. It was a trade, but hardly one that called for a creative eye or an artistic hand. At the time, the basis for both common candles and cheap soap was tallow, or waste animal fat. The ten-year-old had no great interest in working with the slimy spare parts of sheep and other beasts. Inside the shop, the smell of old grease hung in the air like a great soiled sheet. Ben knew that just before his own birth, an older brother, then a toddler, had been killed when he fell into a vat of the boiling tallow. Making candles was boring work: cutting wicks and filling molds. Making soap was worse. Boiling water had to be slowly poured through barrels of wood ashes. This produced a harsh substance called lye. The lye was then mixed with tallow and boiled some more to make bars of crude brown soap.

Fortunately, not all of Ben's time was spent inside the shop. After work, or after church on Sunday, he could find a quiet corner and read. Most of the books in the house were on religion. These the boy found of little value. He already knew that he was a "free thinker." He believed in God, but not necessarily in everything preached from the pulpit of the Old South Church. Then he turned to the classics of the time. He liked *Pilgrim's Progress* so much that he read everything he could find by John Bunyan. He read *Essays to Do Good* by the celebrated Boston minister Cotton Mather. He enjoyed over forty little books in a series called *Historical Collections.* Reading *The Parallel Lives,* a collection of short biographies by the famous Greek author Plutarch, he found "time spent to great advantage." Carl Van Doren, a leading biographer of Franklin, has noted that the best young mind in the colonies "was on the hunt for knowledge and would have found it in a desert."

Outside the house, young Ben Franklin found a world of excitement. Swimming was both his hobby and his pride. The boy took to water as he took to books. He learned to do many tricks in the water, both on the surface and below. One day he asked himself a question: Why couldn't his hands somehow be made larger to allow him to swim faster? He invented a kind of hand paddle made out of

At the age of ten, Ben Franklin began to work in his father's candle-and-soap-making business.

Benjamin Franklin, his father, Josiah Franklin, his mother, Abiah Franklin, and two of his siblings.

wood. These paddles had holes in them for the thumb, much like the palettes that artists use for paint. His invention did work as planned, but they tired his wrists too much to be useful. Ben did better with a feat that required only that he float on the water. Once he and some friends were flying kites near a pond. There was a good wind. Noting the strong pull on the string, Ben wondered if he couldn't float in the water, and let the kite pull him across the lake. A friend carried his clothes around to the other side, and Ben started the mile-long voyage by kite power. He made the trip "without the least fatigue, and with the greatest pleasure." (This ability to float with ease continued to the end of Franklin's life. Even in his seventies, he could amaze people by stretching out in the water and actually going to sleep for half an hour or more.)

Wherever he went, Ben seems to have carried his own excitement with him. There were fish to catch in the rivers and ponds. There were crabs to scramble and splash after in the salt marshes. The boy loved boats. He soon grew to love anything to do with the sea. "When in a boat or canoe with other boys," he later stated, "I was commonly allowed to govern [steer], especially in the case of any difficulty; and upon other occasions I was generally a leader among the boys, and sometimes led them into scrapes."

In an odd kind of way, Ben's love of the sea had a direct effect on the course of his life. Josiah Franklin, as his son later said, was a man of "sound understanding and solid judgment." As Ben turned eleven, and then twelve, the father's sound and solid mind knew just what was happening. Here was a smart boy caught in a dead-end job that he hated. Could Josiah really imagine Ben spending his life stirring hot tallow and cutting wicks? No, surely not. But what would happen to Ben? His father had one big worry: Suddenly Ben would run away, sign on as a ship's cabin boy, and go to sea. This could not be allowed. The father had already lost one son to the sea. Years before, his namesake, Josiah, had sailed off, never to return. Could a second son be sacrificed to the chilly, dark deep? No. But again, what would happen to Ben?

The practical man of solid judgment started taking his youngest son on walks around Boston. Together they watched builders and tradesmen at their jobs. If the soap and candle business was not for Ben, then what did the boy really want to do? Did he want to be a joiner (fine carpenter)? A cooper (barrel maker)? A brazier (metal worker)? A bricklayer? A cutler (knife maker)?

Suddenly the best idea was at hand, ready-made and right in the family. In 1717, Ben's brother James had returned from England. There he had worked as a printer and become an expert. Now, with a press and type brought from London, he had set himself up with a print shop in Boston. Young Ben loved to read and was quick with words. Wouldn't printing be just the right trade for the boy? Why couldn't Ben go to work for his older brother James?

Ben said yes—anything would be better than the grease and the lye. But Josiah Franklin wanted more than just for Ben to go to work for James. Father Franklin knew that more than anything, Ben still wanted to go to sea. For this reason, he asked twelve-year-old Ben to sign a legal paper making him his brother's indentured servant. That meant that Ben's running away would break more than a father's heart. It would also be breaking the law.

"I stood out some time," Benjamin wrote later, "but at last was persuaded, and signed the indentures when I was yet but twelve years old. I was to serve as an apprentice till I was twenty-one years of age, only I was to be allowed journeyman's [skilled worker's] wages during the last year."

A paper of indenture at the time was a standard legal document. The master signed that he would "teach and instruct or cause to be taught or instructed [the particular trade] the best way and manner that he can." Also, the master would provide the servant with "meat, drink, washing, lodging, and all other necessaries." In return, the servant signed that he would serve his master faithfully, day and night, "his secrets keep, his lawful commands everywhere gladly do." The servant had also to agree to other conditions, but these probably made little difference to a twelve-year-old boy: "Taverns, inns, or alehouses he shall not haunt. At cards, dice, tables, or any other unlawful game he shall not play. Matrimony [marriage] he shall not contract...."

Stiff terms, these. But Ben took up the new trade with the eager spirit he carried everywhere. Before long he discovered that he had been born with printer's ink in his veins. Printing would be his business as long as he worked at one. He was to become the best printer in America. And even after gaining fame as a scientist and statesman, he would still be proud of the printer's trade. Writing his last will, the year before he died, he would start out, "I Benjamin Franklin of Philadelphia, printer...."

CHAPTER

2

Alias SILENCE DOGOOD

Nowadays, people are used to a copy machine in every office and an instant print shop on a nearby corner. It is hard for us to imagine what printing was like back in 1718, when Ben Franklin first went to work for his brother James. Today we push buttons. In 1718 they pushed and pulled and lifted and squinted and strained.

In those days printing was essentially two jobs. The first was that of the compositor, who set the type by hand, letter by letter. The second job belonged to the pressman, who operated the crude machine that produced the printed sheets.

The compositor's job required great skill. The type— little metal bars with a letter, number, or punctuation mark cast on one end—was kept in large, shallow wooden cases. Type cases were divided into separate compartments in a standard pattern. This meant that when a compositor reached for an *e,* for instance, he would know automatically right where it was. If the compositor was right-handed, his left hand held what was called a *composing stick.* This was a small metal tray, adjustable for column width. His right hand flew back and forth between the type cases and the composing stick. Letter by letter, line by line, the material to be printed was set in the composing stick. Little grooves and nicks on the pieces of type allowed the compositor to feel his way through the job, again without really thinking about the position of each individual piece. Neither did he have to really think about reaching into the *upper case* for capitals, or into the *lower case* for small letters.

When the compositor had a small block of type in his composing stick, he would transfer it, face up, to a flat surface nearby. Bit by bit, all parts of the printed page were placed in order. Then the type was locked into a heavy metal frame with blocks and wedges of wood. The page was ready for printing when the frame was tight enough to be lifted from the flat surface and carried to the press—but even then the compositor's job was not over. When the printing job was done, the type had to be put back in the cases for future use, again piece by piece.

If that sounds like effort, the job of the pressman perhaps took even more. Inks used at the time required that the paper be at a certain state of dampness—not too dry, not too wet, but "just right." The ink itself had to be not too thick, not too thin, but again "just right." The printing press was the kind of old-fashioned machine that did only part of the work. Printing each page required at least ten separate operations. First the type was inked with a *brayer,* a dabbing device that looked something like a boxing glove on a short stick. Next the sheet of paper to be printed was placed on a flat surface that was hinged to the frame of type. The sheet was held in place with a thin wooden frame that covered the margins. Then it was folded forward onto the type. The frame of type was pushed into the center of the press, and the pressman pulled on a long lever that forced a pressure plate down onto the paper and the type below it. Finally, the whole process was repeated in reverse order, to get the sheet out of the press, and the press ready for another.

This, then, was the trade that Ben Franklin was to follow for the next thirty years. He loved the business. It became his skill, his art at times, his own way to wealth. From the very beginning, it brought him into contact with people who affected his life for the better.

Into the print shop of James Franklin came the apprentices of the best Boston booksellers. Ben made friends easily. He found that he could now borrow books he wanted to read, just as long as he returned them "soon and clean." He sometimes stayed up most of the night reading a book that had to be returned in the morning. Before long he started to read poetry. Soon he was writing ballads, or story poems, of his own. His brother, with an eye to business, encouraged him. When still only twelve years old, Ben wrote a ballad called "The Lighthouse Tragedy." It was based on a recent happening, the sad drowning of a Captain Worthilake and his two daughters. James printed the ballad, and then he sent Ben around town to peddle copies in the street. Because the event was still news, the poem sold well. "This flattered my vanity [pride]," Benjamin later recalled, "but my father discouraged me by ridiculing my performance, and telling me that verse-makers were generally beggars. So I escaped being a poet, most probably a very bad one."

Benjamin Franklin, learning to be a printer.

The practical Josiah Franklin went on to help his youngest son in other ways. At the time, Ben had a good friend named James Collins. Both boys were bright. Both loved to argue. Often they would hit on a subject, then amuse themselves by arguing about it for hours, or even days. One day they found themselves arguing about education for women. Were girls capable of study? Beyond the most basic of basics, should they be sent to school and taught? Franklin said yes. Collins said no. When they parted, Ben felt somewhat defeated. He knew he had the better arguments, but he also realized that Collins was the better talker. Since the two boys could not meet again for a while, Ben put his arguments in writing and sent Collins a letter. Collins replied at once. Before long each had written three or four letters. Quite by accident, Josiah Franklin happened to find this correspondence. He told Ben that although he had the better spelling and punctuation, Collins's writing was much more clear and elegant. Ben's father pointed out several examples, and the boy got the message at once. He made excellence in writing his next goal.

With no teachers to help him, Ben had to teach himself. At the time, one of the most admired English writers was a man named Joseph Addison. Ben got some of Addison's essays. At once he knew that Addison had to be the teacher he lacked. Addison's writing was well organized, clear, and graceful. His choice of words was brilliant. Ben started by going through one of Addison's essays, a sentence at a time. He made very short notes on the subject of each sentence. Those notes he put away for a while, until Addison's exact words had faded from memory. Then he tried to rewrite Addison's essays from the notes, attempting to make his sentences as good as his master's. When Ben had done his best, he would compare his work with the original. In this way he could discover his faults and correct them. To learn organization, he would take an essay by Addison, make his sentence notes on separate scraps of paper, and then jumble the notes. A few weeks later, he would try to put the notes back into the best order and then rewrite the entire essay.

Work in the print shop gave Ben daily lessons in spelling and punctuation. His vocabulary, however, was still limited. To correct this weakness, he invented another self-teaching method. He tried turning Addison's essays into long poems. This forced him to find words that would fit not only the meaning, but also the rhythm and rhyme patterns of the poetic lines. And when the poem was finished, he could gain even more skill by turning it back into prose again.

The agreement signed by both Ben and his brother James had provided the servant with "meat, drink, washing, lodging, and all other necessaries." Before long Ben moved out of his father's crowded house. James Franklin had not yet married. He and his workers lived in a boardinghouse not far from the print shop. Life in the boardinghouse must have been noisy and confusing. But Ben found just the right place to read and study. Early in the morning, and again after work, he could have the whole print shop to himself. Also, now out from under his father's thumb, he didn't have to spend hours in church every Sunday. About this he felt a little guilty, but only a little. Churchgoing, he wrote later, "I still thought a duty, though I could not, as it seemed to me, afford time to practice it."

As the years passed, this boy who could find knowledge in a desert continued the steps in his self-education. Having failed arithmetic in school, he found a textbook and "went through the whole by myself with great ease." Books on navigation taught him geometry. He read philosophy. He read history. He was very impressed with a book called *The Art of Thinking*.

Among the many books that Ben explored during off-duty hours was one called *The Way to Health* by Thomas Tryon. One of Tryon's rules for good health was not to eat meat or fish. Ben experimented with a vegetable diet. He discovered that he felt fine. Loss of meat did not seem to mean loss of vigor or strength. Even though others teased him, he kept at it. Before long Ben suggested to his brother that he stop eating at the boardinghouse. Instead, Ben would be given half the money that James Franklin paid for his food. James agreed to this, and Ben started preparing his own simple meals. He found that he could live on half the money that James gave him. Since Ben received no pay, this meant that he now had a little money to buy books. The plan had another advantage as well. When his fellow workers left the print shop for the big midday meal, Ben could again turn to his books and other interests.

The passing years brought other changes in Ben's life. For one thing, the relationship between the brothers James and Benjamin Franklin slowly grew worse. The eager twelve-year-old apprentice became a hulking teenager with a mind of his own. Ben admitted later that he could be fresh, headstrong, and stubborn. He wanted James to treat him as a brother. But to James, young Ben was a servant, and only that. When trouble broke out between them, one of two things happened. The master would beat the servant, in the typical fashion of the time. Or the brothers would take their quarrel to their father, Josiah

Franklin. On these occasions, the judge's decision usually went to Ben. This only made James even more angry.

James Franklin was a rebel. He disliked the power that a group of ministers had over the daily lives of the people. In fact, James disliked any kind of authority. Whatever the subject, he was usually against the government. He and a group of like-minded friends often met in the shop for hours at a time. They thought of themselves as smart and modern, prophets of the New Age. They roasted the authorities on the flames of their hot words. They called themselves the Hell Fire Club. But what could they really do? How could they change the system?

In 1721 James Franklin decided to start a newspaper. There were already two papers in Boston, but neither, in truth, could be called interesting. The news from faraway Europe was months old by the time it got to Boston. The local news was simply what the government wanted the papers to print. The men who edited these papers had no wish to ruffle the feathers of the officials who ruled the roost. Even the advertisements were boring. One little box about a runaway slave or indentured servant was pretty much like another. Ads for products were simply announcements that such and such was available at such and such a place.

The New England Courant, James Franklin announced, would dare to be different. It would be lively. It would print controversy. It would print opinions. Unlike the other papers, it would never be "VERY, VERY DULL."

With the very first issue, the *Courant* chose sides in the big controversy of the day. At the time, a new wave of the dread disease, smallpox, seemed to be on its way. The argument was over a new and almost untried idea: inoculation, or what today we call a routine smallpox vaccination.

It might be supposed that James Franklin and his friends, young men with independent and modern minds, would have been on the scientific side of the issue. Thus they would have favored inoculation. But no. They were against inoculation because Cotton Mather, the most powerful of the powerful Boston ministers, was for it. Mather was seen as the enemy, and if he favored something, the young rebels were automatically against it.

The *Courant* came out once a week, on Monday, and week by week the battle over inoculation raged on. Someone threw a homemade bomb into Mather's house. It failed to go off, but it made Mather an angry man. He met James Franklin on the street and demanded that the *Courant* stop attacking the good ministers of Boston. "Curses," shouted Mather, "await those that do so!" He went on to state that yes, he did mean the curses of the Lord.

The lively newspaper certainly brightened the days of the fifteen-year-old apprentice named Ben Franklin. When the inoculation argument burned itself out, the *Courant* turned to other issues. Almost every morning, James Franklin's friends gathered in the print shop for an informal meeting. Most of these young men wrote for the paper at times, but they had to be careful. In 1721 there was no such thing as freedom of the press. If a letter or article might displease the government, it was best not to sign your own name to it. James Franklin called himself Timothy Turnstone. The others made up names that were obviously not those of real people: Abigail Afterwit, Harry Meanwell, Fanny Mournful, Ichabod Henroost.

By this time, Ben had finished his course of self-education in the written word. He knew he was ready for publication. But he also knew that his brother would never print in the newspaper anything that he wrote. To James Franklin, Ben was not a brother to be helped but a servant to command.

Still, young Ben was determined to appear in print. Secretly, he wrote a clever, amusing letter to the paper. He copied it over carefully, disguising the handwriting. Finally he reached the end: "Your Humble Servant, SILENCE DO-GOOD." Then, in the dark of the night when no one was around to see, he slipped the letter under the print-shop door.

The next morning, when James Franklin's friends gathered as usual, the Silence Dogood letter was read and discussed. Everyone loved it. From another part of the shop, Ben listened to the conversation. Who could have written the letter? Ben was pleased when only the best minds in Boston were mentioned. He heard James say that he would print the letter in the very next issue. James also liked the writer's promise that more letters would follow.

In Silence Dogood, sixteen-year-old Ben Franklin created a character whose witty, warbling voice still lives in American literature. Silence is her name, not her description. In fact, her constant effort to do good makes her anything but silent. The first two letters give her background. Her personality shines through. "At the time of my birth," she says, "my parents were on shipboard in their way from London to N. England." She goes on to explain "a misfortune, which though I was not then capable of knowing, I shall never be able to forget." Right after her birth, her father died. "As he, poor man, stood upon the deck rejoicing at my birth, a merciless wave entered the ship, and in one moment carried him beyond reprieve [return to safety]. Thus was the first day which I saw, the last that was seen by my father; and thus was my disconsolate [broken-hearted] mother at once made both a parent and a widow."

Obviously, such stuff is not to be taken too seriously. The writer's real purpose is to entertain. Because Silence's mother was so poor, at an early age the child was bound as an apprentice to a country minister. This "pious good-natured young man, a batchelor" spared no effort in bringing the girl up right. Silence was "instructed in all that knowledge and learning which is necessary for our sex." Best of all, "he gave me free use of his library, which though it was but small, yet it was well chose, to inform the understanding rightly and enable the mind to frame great and noble ideas."

Then Silence's mother died. A few years later,

my reverend master... took up a resolution to marry; and having made several unsuccessful fruitless attempts on the more topping sort of our sex, and being tired with making troublesome journeys and visits to no purpose, he began unexpectedly to cast a loving eye upon me, whom he had brought up cleverly....

There is certainly scarce any part of a man's life in which he appears more silly and ridiculous, than when he makes his first onset of courtship. The awkward manner in which my master first discovered [revealed] his intentions, made me, in spite of my reverence to his person, burst out into unmannerly laughter: However, having asked his pardon, and with much ado composed my countenance [calmed my face] I promised him I would take his proposal into serious consideration, and speedily give him an answer.

Here it should be remembered that Franklin's own grand-mother was an indentured servant who grew up to marry her master.

The answer was yes. "Whether it was love, or gratitude, or pride, or all three that made me consent, I know not." And although the marriage caused much gossip in the neighborhood, it was a good one. Seven years passed "in the height of conjugal [married] love and mutual endear-ments." Three children were born. Then the minister died, or according to Silence's soaring words, made "his flight into the Heavenly World." Now, she says, she has some free time to write down her very good opinions in a number of matters. "I never intend to wrap my talent in a napkin," she warns the reader.

As a youngster, Ben Franklin had read Cotton Mather's *Essays to Do Good*. Slowly it now appears that Ben's Dogood letters are his own attempt to write the same book. Silence's opinions on this and that are almost always Franklin's own. She dislikes governments with too much power. She makes fun of Harvard College as a place for young men with more money than brains. She demands equal education for women. Sometimes she just has fun. In one letter, she makes fun of elegies, or poems written to honor the dead. She does this by giving a kind of recipe that will result in a good elegy.

For a good elegy, Silence explains, take a dead person who "went away suddenly, being killed, drowned, or froze to death." Then make a list of all the person's good points. If there are not enough, "borrow some to make up a sufficient quantity: To these add his last words, dying expressions, etc. . . . Then season all with a handful or two of melancholy expressions, such as *dreadful, deadly, cruel cold Death, unhappy fate, weeping eyes,* etc." Add "a sufficient quantity of double rhymes, such as *power, flower; quiver, shiver; grieve us, leave us; tell you, excel you; Expeditions, Physicians; fatigue him, intrigue him;* etc."

As an example of a perfect elegy, Silence offers one written in honor of a "Mrs. Mehitable Kitel of Salem." It is "moving and pathetic," Silence says, "almost beyond comparison." Even today it stands as one of the best bad poems in American literature. Here is a sample:

> Come let us mourn, for we have lost
> a wife, a daughter, and a sister,
> Who has lately taken flight, and
> greatly we have missed her...
> She kissed her husband some little time
> before she expired
> Then leaned her head the pillow on,
> just out of breath and tired.

After the fourteenth Dogood letter, Franklin stopped writing them. He may have run out of ideas. He may have simply got tired of the whole idea. Or more probably, he may have been too busy with other things. By the time letter fourteen was printed, *The New England Courant* was in real trouble, and Ben's duties at the paper had greatly increased.

Since its founding, the *Courant* had been a thorn in the firm hand of the government. In June 1722, James Franklin finally went too far. At the time, pirates were causing increasing trouble for Boston shipping. James Franklin thought the colonial government should be doing more to hunt down the pirate ships. He made up a little news story, a joke about an imaginary ship that might go after the pirates "sometime this month, if wind and weather permit."

James was hauled before the General Court. Immediately he was clapped into jail. He stayed there for a month. During his sentence, Benjamin Franklin took over management of the paper. Then, with James's release, came a worrisome condition. "My brother's discharge," Benjamin wrote later, "was accompanied with an order of the House (a very odd one), that 'James Franklin should no longer print the paper called *The New England Courant.*'"

A problem, and a big one. James's friends gathered for a conference. What about changing the name of the paper? No, that would never do. The government would never accept such a simple trick. Finally it was decided that the paper would in the future be printed under the name Benjamin Franklin, not James Franklin.

There was one big trouble with this idea. Ben Franklin, the brother, was only an indentured servant. As such, he could hardly be the publisher of a popular newspaper. To get around this problem, James Franklin thought of a plan that Ben later called "a very flimsy scheme." James took the old indenture agreement and on the back wrote out a full discharge. This document could be shown to prove that Ben was now a free man. But in secret, James forced Ben to sign new papers that simply continued the old terms.

Relations between the two brothers rapidly went downhill. It did not help when Ben told James that he had written the Dogood papers himself. Even after Ben turned seventeen, James's temper tantrums went on. The beatings continued. Finally it became clear to both that the situation was about to end. How? At first, neither was sure. Ben did feel fairly certain, however, that the new papers of indenture would not cause trouble. James could not reveal them to anyone without also revealing himself as the worst kind of double-dealer.

James Franklin made the rounds of the other six printing shops in Boston. He made sure that none of his competitors would offer Ben a job. This left Ben with only one serious choice. "I then thought of going to New York," he wrote later, "as the nearest place where there was a printer."

Ben knew that his departure from Boston would have to be a kind of escape. If he told anyone about his New York plan, ways would be found to stop him. Also, the captain of any ship going to New York would suspect that a single boy asking for passage was an indentured servant trying to flee his master. For these reasons, Ben told only his old friend James Collins. He had Collins go down to the docks and find the next ship headed for New York. Collins told the captain that he had a friend . . . well, it was like this . . . sometimes girls get pregnant . . . sometimes boys are forced to marry them. Did the captain understand? Would he help a good young fellow in such a fix?

The captain agreed. Ben sold some of his books to get money for the trip. He secretly packed a trunk and just as secretly boarded the ship. Soon it sailed out of Boston Harbor, into the pungent September air of the open sea.

Not long after Ben Franklin had left the Boston paper that was still printed under his name, a small ad appeared in the help-wanted column:

James Franklin, printer in Queen Street, wants a likely lad for an apprentice.

CHAPTER

3

Arrival in Philadelphia

Quick: Make a snap mental picture of Benjamin Franklin. What do you see in your mind's eye?

The picture probably shows a rather old man. He might be described as balding, short, and somewhat pear-shaped. This is the picture created by many artists when Franklin was at the height of his fame—and near the end of his life. But the unknown Ben Franklin who got on the New York boat in the fall of 1723 looked very little like the famous portraits. The seventeen-year-old stood a little over five feet ten. His iron-hard body left no doubt about his strength. He had brown hair, hazel eyes, a straight nose, and thin lips that formed a wide slit of a mouth. People said he was attractive.

Ben took a ship to New York because that was the way people traveled in those days. There was no stagecoach service between Boston and New York. Of course, Ben might have purchased a horse and then followed whatever roads and trails there were. But a horse would have cost money he didn't have. He would also have had to pay for ferry after ferry across the wide Connecticut rivers. No, a ship was the cheapest and easiest way to make the trip.

The journey went well. It took only three days. For the most part, the weather and the winds were good. Once, however, the ship sat on a windless sea off the Rhode Island coast for a few hours. The crew dropped lines over the side, to see what fish were in the area. It happened that many cod were nearby. Ben watched with interest as fish after fish was landed on the deck, cleaned, and then cut up. For some time Ben had opposed the killing of living things for human food. He had been a vegetarian. But he began to change his mind as a huge—and absolutely free!—fish fry got under way. "I had formerly been a great lover of fish," he wrote later, "and, when this came hot out of the frying pan, it smelt admirably well.... I recollected that, when the fish were opened, I saw smaller fish taken out of their stomachs; then thought I: 'If you eat one another, I don't see why we mayn't eat you.' So I dined on fish very heartily."

That much the seventeen-year-old might have written. But the older man who wrote the account from memory chose to add, "So convenient a thing it is to be a reasonable creature, since it enables one to find or make a reason for everything one has a mind to do."

That was the end of Ben Franklin the vegetarian. He sailed on to New York, got off the boat, and found a city that looked quite unlike his native Boston. At the time the different colonies in the New World were quite unlike one another, and they all had more contact with London than they did with each other. New York was only half the size of

Boston, but it was much more of an international city. It had been founded by the Dutch, and the tall, narrow Dutch houses looked little like the English houses in Boston. Many of the people were of Dutch descent. They mingled with the English and also with the Huguenots, French Protestants who had fled their country for religious reasons. There were also Jews in the city, as well as people from the West Indies and other parts of the world. On the streets as many as eighteen languages could be heard in a short time.

Ben was not to stay in New York for long. He quickly learned that the only printer in town was a man named William Bradford. Going to Bradford's shop, he found that the printer needed no help at the time. But Bradford was a kind man. He told Ben that his son, Andrew Bradford, had recently opened a print shop in Philadelphia. The son had just lost a good printer, and he probably needed a replacement. Franklin had already come all the way from Boston. Why didn't he continue the hundred miles to Philadelphia and seek work there?

There were ships that sailed to Philadelphia, but Ben had little money left. He learned that the cheapest way to make the trip would be to take a ferry across the Hudson River, walk across New Jersey, then take a boat down the Delaware River to Philadelphia. He took his trunk to a shipping company that would send it the long way around by water. Then, with his pockets stuffed with a few light clothes, he sought out the ferry.

In his *Autobiography*, Franklin describes his trip to Philadelphia in some detail. It shows how hard travel could be back in 1723. The ferry to New Jersey turned out to be a small sailboat, mostly open to the weather, with little cover for the few passengers it could carry. Ben paid his fee and climbed aboard. The boat set out for its destination, Perth Amboy, New Jersey. But soon a bad storm came up. The wind, Franklin later wrote, "tore our rotten sails to pieces." Even worse, the wind was blowing in the wrong direction. Instead of moving forward to New Jersey, the little boat was driven back across New York Harbor toward the Long Island shore. And even worse than that, another passenger, a Dutchman, had come aboard with a large bottle of spirits as a traveling companion. The Dutchman became more and more tipsy and finally fell overboard. Just before he sank, Ben reached out and managed to catch hold of his hair. The drunk was pulled back into the boat, where he soon went to sleep.

For the rest of the company, however, the horrors went on. Before long they heard a loud noise. Peering through the spray, they saw the surf beating on the Long Island shore. The coast was rocky; there was no place to land. The boatman had no choice but to throw out the anchor, to keep the small ship off the rocks. A few Long Islanders walked down to the water's edge and shouted out to the boat. Ben and the others shouted back. There were canoes in sight. Couldn't the people on the boat be rescued? But the howling wind and roaring surf drowned out the sound of voices. Or, perhaps, the people on shore knew what was wanted, but dared not take the chance.

Darkness began to fall, and the people on the boat soon knew where they would have to spend the night. Soaked to the skin, they huddled up where they could and tried to sleep. This proved impossible. The waves were still high, and salt spray showered down into the boat all night long.

The next morning the sea calmed down, and the wind

changed. The boatman set what remained of the sails for Perth Amboy, New Jersey. The trip was a slow one. It took nearly all day. By the time Ben stumbled ashore, he had been thirty hours on the open water—without sleep, without food, without drink but a swig of "filthy rum." More than that, he was feverish. He knew what he looked like: an unshaven, dirty, damp mess of a boy who might easily be picked up as an escaped indentured servant. He walked a little way and found a place to stay. Remembering that cold water was supposed to be good for a fever, he gulped swallow after swallow before he collapsed into bed. Still, he "sweat plentiful most of the night."

In the morning Ben woke up feeling better. His fever had left him. He felt good enough to start the fifty-mile walk across New Jersey. The only trouble was that soon a hard rain started. By noon, drenched for hours, he knew he could walk no farther. In his own words, he was "beginning now to wish that I had never left home." He came to a tumbledown inn that looked like a cheap place to stay. Again he fell into bed exhausted.

Another morning: another day. This proved to be a better one. By evening, Ben was only ten miles from Burlington, New Jersey, a town above Philadelphia on the Delaware River. The inn at which he stopped was run by a now-and-then physician who introduced himself as Dr. Brown. "He entered into conversation with me while I took some refreshment," Franklin wrote later, "and, finding I had read a little, became very sociable and friendly." Ben's sleep that night must have been a good one, and the next day promised to be even better.

Bidding farewell to Dr. Brown, Ben quickly walked the ten miles to Burlington. He asked about the boats that took passengers downriver to Philadelphia. Unfortunately, he had just missed one. This was a Saturday. The next boat would be on Tuesday.

Ben was stunned. The long trip from Boston to New York had taken him only three days. The much shorter trip from New York to Philadelphia had already taken much longer. The first night had been spent in an open boat. The second night he had been feverish. The third night was really half a day and a night, spent in utter collapse. The fourth had been spent with Dr. Brown. Now it looked as though three more nights would have to be spent in Burlington. This was not the only problem. A place to stay would cost money, and Ben was down to his last few coins.

Later that evening, out for a stroll, Ben saw a small boat making its way down the Delaware River. Some of the people on board were rowing. Could it be? Could the boat be headed for Philadelphia? Ben shouted to the passengers, and they yelled back. Yes, they did hope to make Philadelphia that very night. And even better, they would take Ben on board if he would help with the rowing.

Ben pulled on a heavy oar until dusk came, and then darkness. The passengers squinted into the gloom, looking for the lights that might mark Philadelphia. Midnight came. Had they passed the city? No one could be sure. But if they had, rowing farther would make no sense at all. The best plan seemed to head into a little creek nearby where they could get out and spend the night on land. This they did. It was cold for early October, and no one wanted to spend the hours till sunup shivering on the damp ground. Some of the passengers ripped a farmer's rail fence apart to make a fire. Its light and heat helped to pass the hours till dawn.

In the morning the little company rowed out of the

creek, back into the Delaware River. There was Phila-delphia!—spread out right below them. Ben soon climbed out of the boat at the Market Street wharf, said farewell to the others, and walked into the city he would one day be able to claim almost as his own.

In 1723 Philadelphia was larger than New York but smaller than Boston. Philadelphia was also very different from Boston. More of the houses were of solid brick. The streets were wider, and laid out in a regular gridiron pattern. It was about nine on a Sunday morning, and the city was quiet. Ben was very aware of his poor appearance. He still worried about being picked up as a runaway indentured servant. If that happened, how could he prove otherwise? He was seventeen years old. He had no job. He knew absolutely nobody in the city. And as for money, he was down to his last Dutch dollar—exactly.

Seeing a boy carrying some bread made Ben realize that he was also very hungry. He learned from the boy that a bakery on Second Street was open. Hurrying to the shop, he went in and asked for a biscuit. This confused the baker; *biscuit* was a Boston term, not a word used in Phila-delphia. Then he asked for a *three-penny loaf*. Again, the baker didn't know what was wanted. Finally Ben asked for three cents' worth of anything. The baker amazed him by producing three huge puffy rolls. This was more than Ben expected; the solid coins of Philadelphia would evidently buy more than the paper money of Boston.

What followed must be expressed in Franklin's well-known words:

> I was surprised at the quantity, but took it, and, having no room in my pockets, walked off with a roll under each arm, and eating the other. Thus I went up Market

Street as far as Fourth Street, passing by the door of Mr. Read, my future wife's father; when she, standing at the door, saw me, and thought I made, as I certainly did, a most awkward, ridiculous appearance.

Ben wandered through a few more streets, munching on the roll. Then, feeling thirsty, he returned to the river for a drink. The roll was now gone; it was a meal in itself. Ben gave the other two to a woman and her child, who had come down the river with him and were now waiting for another boat to take them farther. Heading back into town, he noticed that the streets were filling with people, clean-scrubbed and in their Sunday best. All seemed to be going in the same direction. He joined them. Soon he found himself sitting on a bench in a Quaker meeting-house. He did not know that the Quaker religious service would be held without a minister. (Then as now, at a Quaker meeting, people sit silently unless they feel called upon to speak.) Ben was worn out from the rowing, drowsy from the short night spent by the campfire. "I fell fast asleep," he wrote later, "and continued so till the meeting broke up, when one was kind enough to rouse me. This was, therefore, the first house I was in or slept in, in Philadelphia."

Back on the street, Ben looked around for an inn, where he could continue his sleep. He passed one with a sign: The Three Mariners. Should he enter? Something held him back. He turned for advice to a young Quaker man whose face he liked. No, the man said. The Three Mariners was not really a respectable place. "If thee will walk with me, I'll show thee a better."

Soon after, at the Crooked Billet, Ben ate a good meal, was shown to a bed, and fell down on it in his dirty clothes.

This nineteenth-century engraving depicts seventeen-year-old Franklin on his first day in Philadelphia in 1723. Deborah Read, who would marry him years later, watches from a doorway as Ben carries some just-purchased rolls.

At six he was awakened for supper, then he went back to
sleep. He was now more than five days removed from New
York, and more than a week from Boston. Until his trunk
arrived by boat, he would be forced to look like a tramp.
He was a very young man in a strange city, with no money
and no job. How would Philadelphia treat him?

The next day would tell.

CHAPTER

4

A Continuing Education

Monday morning the first thing, Ben tried to clean himself up as best he could. Then he left the Crooked Billet and made his way to the print shop of Andrew Bradford. This had been his destination for six days.

Like his father, William, in New York, Andrew Bradford had no work for the young printer. But like his father also, he was a kind man. He gave Ben breakfast. He promised him what work might come along in the future. He even offered to board Ben in his own house until the boy could put his new life in order. Meanwhile, he suggested that Ben pay a call on a man named Samuel Keimer. He had heard that Keimer was about to open a print shop on Market Street. The new printer might need some good help to get started.

Ben found Keimer's shop on Market Street and went

in. He found a man of about forty. Keimer peered at the boy from above a long beard that he never cut. His clothes were hardly tidy. Clearly, Keimer was what Ben later called him, an "odd fish" of a man. Nevertheless, Keimer proved to be talkative and friendly. Yes, he said, he might have some work very soon. He put a composing stick in Ben's hand to test his skill. Yes, he said again with a nod. He explained that he was in the process of writing an elegy on the death of a well-known young Philadelphian. When the elegy was finished, Ben could help print it.

Could Ben help to set the elegy in type? No, that was not possible. Keimer was a truly original kind of poet: he composed his lines right on a composing stick. He wrote nothing out first for a compositor to copy. But Ben could, if he wanted to, try to put his old printing press in order. Keimer was just setting up shop, and he had never used the press. In fact, although he was a good compositor, he knew little about presswork.

Ben thought Keimer a rather strange man, but he was in no position to be particular. In the days that followed, he put Keimer's creaking press in working condition. Bradford offered him a few little jobs. Then Keimer's elegy was ready, and Ben ran off the copies. Keimer got a small pamphlet to print, and Ben's employment began to look more secure. Meanwhile, his trunk had arrived by boat. He now had his favorite books at hand in the evening and a choice of clothes in the morning.

Samuel Keimer did not like it that Ben continued to board in the home of Andrew Bradford. The reason was clear: Bradford was Keimer's competitor in business. Keimer arranged for Ben to stay with Mr. and Mrs. John Read, who owned the house next to his Market Street shop. The Read's daughter, Deborah, was the girl who had stood on

the stoop and watched Franklin's undistinguished arrival in Philadelphia. Ben was now a young man on his way
up, and Debby—as he soon learned to call her—was nearly
his age.

Seven years later, Debby and Ben were to marry each
other. But it was hardly love at first sight. Now Ben pre-
ferred to spend his free time with young friends who had
done some reading and liked to talk about ideas. He
worked hard and spent little. He kept out of places like
The Three Mariners. He already thought that if he could
open his own shop someday, he could beat out both Bradford and Keimer. Bradford, in Ben's opinion, had little real
interest in the business. Bradford also had little ability
with the English language. (In those days even people who
could read fairly well often spelled by ear. The good
printer was the one who could make corrections as he
went along.) And as for Keimer, well, such an "odd fish"
was bound to have trouble in a city where most of the
business came from somber, serious Quakers.

As the months passed, Philadelphia slowly became
home as Ben tried to forget Boston. Not since his arrival
had he written a word to his family. Legally, he was still an
indentured servant on the run, and he did not entirely
trust his brother James. Who knew what James might try to
do, just out of spite?

Then one day an unexpected letter arrived. A brother-
in-law of Ben's was a sea captain named Robert Holmes.
The ship that Holmes commanded made regular runs
between Boston and New Castle, a Delaware port forty
miles downriver from Philadelphia. Holmes happened to
hear that a young printer named Franklin had recently
arrived in Philadelphia. It could only be Ben. He wrote
Ben a letter, begging him to return home. Whatever had

gone wrong in Boston, he stated, would be made right again once Ben went back. He had seen Ben's family. He knew their distress.

Ben replied at once to the letter from Captain Holmes. As best he could, he set forth his reasons for leaving home and wishing to stay where he was. Then came a stroke of luck. When Holmes received Ben's letter in New Castle, he happened to be in conversation with Governor William Keith of Pennsylvania. Holmes told Governor Keith about the young printer and let him read the letter. Keith was amazed—at Franklin's ability to write so well, at his obvious promise as a printer, at his age. The printers already in Philadelphia, Sir William Keith explained to Captain Holmes, were "wretched ones." If this young Franklin could do any better, he should be encouraged. In fact, Keith was ready to hand over all of Pennsylvania's official printing to any new printer who could do the job well.

All this, of course, Ben knew nothing about. So he was completely surprised when, a few days later, Sir William Keith arrived at Keimer's Market Street shop. Hearing something happening on the street outside, both Samuel Keimer and Ben Franklin looked out of a second-floor window. Why, there was Sir William Keith! Keith was accompanied by an aide. As the two made their way toward the print-shop door, Keimer dashed down the stairs. Why was the governor paying him a call?

Then Samuel Keimer learned the sad news. Sir William Keith wanted to see Ben Franklin, not Keimer himself. Well, Franklin was upstairs. No problem. Governor Keith climbed the stairs and told Ben that he was so glad to make his acquaintance. The compliments flowed like wine. Soon Keith suggested that they go to a Third Street tavern, where, he had heard, there was an excellent wine to be tasted. Ben could hardly refuse. Before long Franklin and Governor Keith were off, leaving Samuel Keimer standing there, in Ben's words, "like a pig poisoned."

The meeting was a good one. Over the well-tasted wine, Governor Keith suggested that Franklin set himself up in business. By doing so, the young man could provide good printing not only for the government, but also for anyone who wanted it. Ben hung back at first. He had recently arrived in Philadelphia, and he had little money. A good printing press and several sets of type would cost a lot.

As for money, responded Keith, what about your father? It was common practice in those days for fathers to set sons up in business. Governor Keith knew that Ben's father owned a successful candle-and-soap shop in Boston. Ben agreed to go to Boston, face the father he had deserted, and ask for money.

The agreement between Governor Keith and Franklin had to be kept secret. If Keimer learned that his employee intended to set up shop for himself, Ben would be out of a job. He told Keimer only that he wanted time off to visit his family in Massachusetts. Then some time passed before a ship left for Boston. "I went on working with Keimer as usual," Franklin wrote later, "the governor sending for me now and then to dine with him, a very great honor I thought it, and conversing with me in the most affable [cordial], familiar, and friendly manner imaginable."

Toward the end of April 1724, Ben boarded a ship for Boston. The trip took two weeks. Captain Holmes had not been to Boston since the exchange of letters with Ben. Neither had he written that he knew where Ben was. Ben's sudden arrival took his family by surprise. But everyone was overjoyed to see him again—everyone but brother

James, that is. When Ben walked into the print shop where he had worked for five years, James's greeting was more like a grudge. He looked Ben over and returned at once to his work. Ben was dressed in a splendid new suit, and if James wanted to continue the old quarrel, well, Ben was more than willing. He turned to James's workers with a smile. They were curious, so Ben told them all about wonderful Philadelphia, and how happy he was in his new employment. He produced an expensive watch that was the envy of all. Then came a great display of silver coins. Finally, leaving the men some change for a drink after work, he turned on his heels and walked out of the shop.

"Sullen" was Ben's word for James's reaction. James later told their mother that Ben "had insulted him in such a manner before his people that he could never forget or forgive it."

Having evened the score with his brother, Ben turned to Josiah Franklin with the purpose of his trip. When his son handed him a personal letter from Sir William Keith, governor of Pennsylvania, Josiah was much impressed. He was even more impressed by Keith's high praise of Ben. The governor was sure that there was a fortune to be made in Philadelphia printing. Josiah, however, was still a very cautious, very practical man. After all, Ben had hardly turned eighteen. In Josiah's opinion, no eighteen-year-old had the good judgment to be "trusted with the management of a business so important, and for which the preparation must be so expensive." The idea itself was a good one—but not yet. If Ben would work hard and save money until he was twenty-one, Josiah would be glad to help out. Not now.

Ben was disappointed, of course. But he could see his father's point of view, and the two parted friends. It had been good to see his parents again. It had also been good to see James Collins, his oldest and best friend. In fact, Collins had been so taken by Ben's account of Philadelphia that he decided to make the move himself. He would accompany Ben on the return trip. Then, learning that Ben wanted to stop at Newport, Rhode Island, to visit his brother John, Collins decided to go on ahead and wait for Ben in New York. He left his books to be boxed up with some of Ben's and departed.

In Newport, Ben had a good visit with John and his family. He agreed to do John a favor. A friend of John's, a man named Vernon, was owed some money by a person who lived near Philadelphia. A lot of money, in fact, about thirty-five pounds. (This would have been the better part of a working man's wages for a year.) John asked Ben to get the money if he could, then hold it until Vernon sent him instructions as to how to send it. Ben promised to do his best.

On the sail from Newport to New York, an incident occurred that sheds light on Ben's character at the time. As he always did, Ben grew friendly with the other passengers. One was a serious, sensible older Quaker woman who seemed to take a kind of motherly interest in the boy. Also on board were two young women who constantly flirted with Ben. The Quaker woman grew alarmed when she saw Ben's growing attraction. She took him aside. "Young man," she began, "I am concerned for thee, as thou has no friend with thee, and seems not to know much of the world." In short, these were "very bad women"—just the sort an upright young man must learn to stay away from. Ben took her advice to heart. When the ship docked in New York, the girls gave him their address and asked him to pay a visit. He had no intention of doing so.

But the young women did receive a visit of another kind. Soon after they left the ship, the captain noticed that a silver spoon and some other items were missing from his cabin. He suspected the young women, and Ben had the address. A search warrant was issued, and the captain soon found the stolen goods. The young women were properly punished.

Ben had escaped getting involved with the two women, but bad news of another kind awaited him in New York. During Ben's seven-month absence from Boston, Collins had started to drink—first a little, then a lot. Now, out in the world on his own, he had fallen into an alcoholic pit. (In the eighteenth century, alcoholism was generally not viewed as a disease but as a character flaw.) Ben learned that Collins had been drunk every day since his arrival in New York. Moreover, Collins had gambled away all his money, and then some. Before they left town, Ben had to pay Collins's hotel bill. He also had to pay his friend's fare to Philadelphia. Then he had to pay Collins's room and board while he looked for a job.

Because of his habit, Collins couldn't find a job. It made things worse that Franklin was successful in getting Vernon's money. Collins knew that Ben had cash at hand, lots of it. He was always borrowing, borrowing, borrowing. This troubled Ben. Suppose Vernon sent for his money. Ben just didn't have it. All he had were Collins's many promises to repay. Now Ben began to think that perhaps his father had been right, after all. Maybe an eighteen-year-old just didn't have good sense when it came to money matters.

Franklin's relationship with Collins grew worse and worse. His onetime friend was now a care and a constant annoyance. One day both young men were rowing with some friends on the Delaware River. Collins, as often happened, had consumed too much alcohol. He refused to take his turn at the oars. "I will be rowed home," the drunk said.

"We will not row you," Franklin maintained.

"You must," Collins replied, "or stay all night on the water."

Franklin was as furious at Collins as he had ever been. The others tried to talk him out of it, but Franklin insisted that no one row until Collins had taken his turn. Time passed, the boat slowly drifting downstream. Collins, crazily drunk and seized with a rage he could not control, demanded that Franklin get behind the oars and row them home. No, Franklin stated, Collins should row. Well, Collins said, if Franklin would not row willingly, he would make him row. He stood up in the boat and staggered toward Franklin. He threw a punch. Franklin easily managed to get a hold on Collins and throw him headlong into the river.

Collins was a good swimmer, and Franklin knew that even drunk, he was in no real danger. The others began to row the boat slowly away from Collins. The swimmer tried to reach it, but whenever he got close, they would pull the boat just a little farther away. Would Collins now agree to row if they let him into the boat? No! The game kept up until Collins was truly exhausted. Only then did they lift him into the boat and row him home dripping wet.

This ended things between Ben Franklin and James Collins. Soon after, Collins met a sea captain from the West Indies. The captain had been asked by a wealthy man on the island of Barbados to find a private tutor for his sons. Collins agreed to take the job and promised to repay Ben with the first money he earned. He sailed off to the

West Indies, and Franklin never heard from him again.

Meanwhile, Ben had returned to Keimer's shop. Although Keimer was about twice Franklin's age, the two developed an odd kind of friendship. Samuel Keimer was a strange man, but Ben rather enjoyed his strangeness. Keimer never cut his beard. He kept Saturday as his Sunday. In an age of early marriages and big families, he lived alone. He was forever interesting himself in weird new ideas and odd religions. Ben enjoyed arguing with Keimer in the shop. He found that if he argued indirectly and planned his questions carefully, he could easily catch the older man in a logical trap. Soon Keimer would not answer the most innocent-sounding question without first demanding what Franklin intended to do with the answer. The two socialized after hours as well. On at least one occasion they cooked a meal and entertained two young ladies in Keimer's house.

Before long Keimer suggested that the two men start a new religious sect. Keimer himself would decide what the doctrines were to be, then preach them to all comers. Franklin would argue with anyone who wanted to disagree. Keimer asked Franklin to grow a beard and honor Saturday as the holy day. Mostly for fun, Ben agreed—but only on the condition that one of the doctrines of the new sect be the non-eating of meat. Ben knew that more than anything, Keimer loved to eat. The older man agreed, but hardly with enthusiasm. For three months, in Franklin's words, "poor Keimer suffered." Then his stomach became once again his master. He gave up the new sect and ordered a young pig for a roast. Franklin and some friends were invited to a feast. But the pig was ready too soon. Keimer devoured the whole thing before the company arrived.

Ben had other friends that he took more seriously than Samuel Keimer. One was a young man named James Ralph. Unlike Franklin, Ralph was a married man; he even had a small child. But very much like Franklin, Ralph loved to read and to discuss ideas. Ralph was clever, polite, and gifted with words. "I think I never knew a prettier talker," Franklin wrote later. Ralph spent his days working as a clerk for a Philadelphia merchant, but his real interest lay in poetry. With two other friends, Franklin and Ralph often spent their Sundays by the peaceful Schuylkill River. There they would read to each other, then talk about what they had read.

A friend of a quite different kind was Sir William Keith. Even though Franklin's father had turned him down, Governor Keith's invitations and meals continued. So did the governor's desire to see Benjamin Franklin have a print shop of his own. Josiah Franklin had been wrong about Ben, the governor believed. Good sense did not always have to wait for advancing years. "And since he will not set you up," Keith stated one day, "I will do it myself. Give me an inventory [list] of the things necessary to be had from England, and I will send for them. You shall repay me when you are able; I am resolved to have a good printer here, and I am sure you must succeed."

Franklin did not mind this kind of flattery. He knew he could become the best printer in Philadelphia, if only he had the equipment. He quickly prepared a list. The cost would be about a hundred pounds (some $40,000 in our money today). Then he returned to Keith—only to find that the governor had upped the offer. Wouldn't it make better sense, the older man asked, for Franklin to go to England himself? If Ben went to London, he could be right there to choose everything he needed. The equipment would be better, and so would the cost. Also, Franklin could see what additional business might be had as a seller of books and stationery. Ben had to agree that the governor's offer made a lot of sense.

"Then," said Sir William Keith, "get yourself ready to go with *Annis.*" This was the only ship that regularly sailed between Philadelphia and London. However, the *Annis* would not be leaving Philadelphia for several months. As before, Ben's plans had to be kept secret. Samuel Keimer could not learn that his skillful pressman was about to go head-to-head with him in business.

But Ben did tell a few people whom he trusted. For one, he told James Ralph. Before long, Ralph confessed to Franklin that he had a secret plan of his own. He, too, would abandon his employer. He was tired of being a clerk for a merchant. Why not be a merchant himself? He would go with Franklin to London. There he could make contacts with businessmen who might send him goods to sell on commission, or part of the profits. Of course, Ben was glad to have the company.

Another person Ben told was Deborah Read. By now, the long friendship between Ben and Debby had ripened into something approaching love. Then it was love. Under normal circumstances, Ben and Debby would have been married in the fall of 1724. But things were not normal. Debby's father, John Read, had died in July. Mrs. Read was not ready to let Debby go. Also, Ben was about to set sail for London, then return. Any cross-Atlantic voyage was something of a danger. Why not wait until Ben had returned from England and set himself up in business? The two young people agreed. Ben "interchanged some promises with Miss Read" and prepared to depart for England.

As October glory spread itself over the Pennsylvania hills, Ben's plans were clear. The *Annis* would soon sail for London. He would be aboard, with his good friend James Ralph. He would kiss his fiancée, Debby, good-bye, both of them knowing that he would sail back on the very next ship. And he would return not only to marry Debby, but to become the best printer in Pennsylvania.

CHAPTER

5

To England and Back

In the modern age, millions of passengers cross the Atlantic every year. They travel by air. Those with enough money and style choose the Concorde, the plane that makes the trip in about four hours. Before the jet airplane, the fastest diesel-powered ship took about four days. But back in Franklin's time, the only power was wind power. A good time was not four hours or four days but four weeks. A trip could take more like four months. Shipping schedules depended on the whim of the winds. In advance, no one could be certain when a ship would leave one side of the Atlantic or arrive at the other.

Time was not the only problem that Franklin faced on his trip to London. Like the little *Annis*—and all ships were little—most boats carried both passengers and freight. The passenger cabin was always damp, cold in the winter and hot in the summer. Since seawater is salty and undrinkable, all water for human use had to be carried in barrels. Drinking water was carefully watched; bathing was secondary and often ignored. Toilet facilities were primitive. The ship provided transportation only, not personal care, amusement, or even food. Passengers had to pack their own provisions, called stores, before leaving. The usual diet was salted meat or fish, dried fruit, and the kind of gum-raking fare still called sea biscuits. After a long ocean voyage, it was not unusual for passengers to leave the ship undernourished, limp from lack of exercise, and in need of care.

Of course, Franklin knew in advance what the trip would be like. His chief concern was that he lacked certain documents. Governor Keith had promised him letters of recommendation to several important people in London. Keith had also promised letters of credit, or papers that would let Franklin purchase equipment in the governor's name. But as the time came for the *Annis* to leave Philadelphia, Franklin had still not received the letters. More than once he had called at the governor's office. Each time he had been told that Sir William was tied up with important business, then given a date on which to return. Finally, on his last call, Franklin had been told by a secretary not to worry. He should board the *Annis* and sail downriver to the next port of call, New Castle, Delaware. The governor himself would be at New Castle with the papers ready.

This Franklin did. He and James Ralph got on the boat and found their place in steerage—not the passenger cabin but a dim, damp, and airless area below the main deck. When they arrived at New Castle, Governor Keith was nowhere to be seen. Franklin learned where the governor was staying and paid still another call. Once more he was met by the secretary. Again he was told that the governor was too busy to see him. But again: not to worry. Governor Keith would send the papers to the ship before it sailed. He sent warm wishes, hopes for a good trip, and prayers for a speedy return.

Franklin returned to the *Annis*, not without worry. These were lifted when he saw Colonel French, the governor's personal aide, coming on board. The colonel greeted people and did business here and there. Franklin had no doubt that French had delivered the letters to the captain, especially when the colonel approached him with more of the governor's warm wishes, fond hopes, and heartfelt prayers.

During the time Colonel French was on board, Franklin was distracted by events that turned out to be good news. One of the passengers in the master cabin was a famous Philadelphia lawyer named Andrew Hamilton. He was traveling to England with his son. At New Castle, however, Hamilton received word that his legal services had been requested at home. The case involved a seized ship, and the fee was too much for Hamilton to resist. He and his son abandoned the trip at once, returning to Philadelphia in a great hurry. About the same time, the other passengers in the cabin noticed all the fuss that Colonel French was making over the young man Franklin. They decided that Franklin and his friend Ralph must be gentlemen of quality. The two were invited into the cabin, to take the places of the Hamiltons. Better than that, lawyer Hamilton and his son had left their plentiful stores on board, which were enjoyed by all.

When the ship was under way, Franklin asked the captain for the letters. He was told that all important mail had been put into a bag together for safekeeping. The captain would not open the bag until they neared London.

Franklin was not too concerned. The company in the master cabin was excellent. As usual, Franklin made friends quickly. He especially liked Thomas Denham, a Quaker merchant who was going to London to buy goods for resale in Philadelphia. The voyage took exactly seven weeks, and the *Annis* docked in London on Christmas Eve, 1724.

But when the captain's mailbag was opened, the expected letters were not to be found. Franklin was shocked. What had happened? He turned to Thomas Denham, an older man with a wealth of experience. Denham was not at all surprised. Sir William Keith, he explained, was, all in all, a good man. He was also a good governor. But he had one bad habit. He often made promises that he was unable to fulfill. "He wished to please everybody," Franklin wrote later, "and, having little to give, he gave expectations." Denham laughed at the idea of a letter of credit from Sir William. In truth, Keith was not a wealthy man; he had no credit to give. Franklin realized that if he had not had to keep his trip a secret, he would have learned about Keith's weakness much sooner.

Now it was too late. He and James Ralph were stranded in London. Neither had money for the return passage to Philadelphia. Neither knew much about job possibilities in London. But they were the best of friends; they stuck together. They found cheap rooms in the Little Britain section of the city. They stuck together even after Ralph dropped his bombshell. He now told Franklin that he had no intention of ever returning to America. He had come to London to launch his career in the arts, he said. As for his wife and child, well, they were part of his past. Her parents, whom he disliked anyhow, had money enough to support them.

Both young men set out to find work. Franklin was lucky. He had a trade. He could easily show his skill as a printer. In a few days, he had a job at Palmer's, one of the biggest printing companies in London. But James Ralph, though well-read and intelligent, had no marketable skill. Also, his hopes were much too high. Trying for work as an actor, he was shunned. Then he tried writing essays like Joseph Addison's. No success there either. Finally he offered his services doing any kind of writing. He would even copy legal documents for lawyers. Months passed, and still no job.

Meanwhile both young men lived on Franklin's good wages. There was some money left over for plays, music, and the other amusements that youth can always find in a large city. Even though Ralph's debt to Franklin rose and rose, the two friends enjoyed each other's company. They liked having fun together. Franklin was now nineteen. As James Ralph forgot about his wife and child, Franklin found himself forgetting about his engagement to Deborah Read. He wrote her a letter saying that he could not come home right away. That was all. He never wrote Debby again.

Busy London offered many temptations, and at times Franklin could not say no. Where once he had avoided taverns, now he delighted in eating and drinking there with friends. He learned the sad results of too much food and wine. He tried to control his behavior, often without success. In his own words, he "went on sinning more freely than ever." He was also troubled by what he called his "intrigues [illegal affairs] with low women."

Yet the serious side of Franklin's nature never left him. His conscience prodded him to the point of pain. He began to ask himself why he was behaving as he was. For that matter, why did people in general behave as they did? Why had James Ralph deserted his wife to seek fame as a writer? Why was he, Franklin, unable to leave his tavern companions and the bar girls? He sought help from books. He did a great deal of reading. Slowly he began to believe that, in truth, people could not control their own behavior. Human beings were like machines, he thought. All people were part of the greatest machine of all, the universe. In the universe, physical laws determined what happened. The universe was not governed by notions of right or wrong, good or bad. It was the same way with people. Regardless of what they thought, they acted only to avoid pain and seek pleasure. They had to act in the way they did.

When Franklin had his thoughts in order, he started putting them down on paper. The final result he called by the lofty title "A Dissertation [essay] on Liberty and Necessity, Pleasure and Pain." At Palmer's print shop, he set his essay in type and ran off a few hundred copies. Those that circulated brought him into contact with other free thinkers of London, some of them famous men. Then he had second thoughts. His practical, calculating mind took over once again. What would it do to his career to be labeled an atheist, or unbeliever? In an era when many people put their trust in God, it was hardly fashionable to trust a pleasure-pain principle as the sole ruler over human life. Franklin regretted writing the pamphlet, and he destroyed all the copies that were left.

Meanwhile, James Ralph was giving Franklin his own demonstration of the pleasure-pain principle. Ralph avoided the pain of hard work by remaining unemployed. And as for pleasure, he took up with an attractive, intelligent young widow who lived in the same building. Mrs. T

57

was a milliner, or maker and seller of hats. (Franklin did not spell out her full name in his writings.) She had a shop, and she made enough money to support herself and a young child. But when Ralph moved in with her, her income was not enough. Ralph now had to either find a job or lose the milliner.

He chose the first course. The job he found was that of a country schoolmaster, at some distance from London. At first this looked like a good solution to Ralph's problems. He could slowly begin to repay the twenty-seven pounds he had borrowed from Franklin during the past year. Meanwhile, he could visit the milliner whenever possible. But Mrs. T's relationship with Ralph had displeased many of her customers. Her millinery business went down. Needing money, she came to Franklin, again and again. Franklin completely misread the charming young widow. He began to think he could take Ralph's place in her life. In his own words, he "attempted familiarities." Suddenly one day, she flashed into sudden fury. Not only that, she told Ralph what had happened. Now it was Ralph's words that were bitter and angry. He told Franklin that the matter ended their friendship. It also ended any debt that Franklin might imagine he was owed. Franklin had done him dirt. Well, he could play dirty, too.

James Ralph was right. The friendship was over. Franklin never received a single penny of the twenty-seven pounds.

Now Franklin was really determined to save enough money to pay his passage home. To this end, he found a cheaper place to live. He also found a job with another large printing house, Watts's. The new job paid more money. In his new location, he could avoid his old tavern friends. He could become a saver, not a spender.

Employing more than fifty people, the Watts printing

house was even bigger than Palmer's. Franklin was horrified to find that nearly all the workers drank beer, lots of it, all day long. "My companion at the press," he wrote later, "drank every day a pint before breakfast, a pint at breakfast with his bread and cheese, a pint between breakfast and dinner, a pint at dinner, a pint in the afternoon about six o'clock, and another when he had done his day's work." When Franklin asked the men why they drank so much, they replied that they had to. Presswork was hard work. It took strength. They told Franklin, a man had "to drink strong beer, that he might be strong to labor."

This was rubbish, Franklin thought. He himself did not drink on the job, and everyone knew that he was the only pressman who regularly carried two frames of type, not one, up the stairs. He told the others that the only nourishment in beer came from the grain used to make it. A little cheap bread would provide the same amount of muscle power. Why did the pressmen go on, year after year, spending a quarter of their wages on beer?

The twenty-year-old from the colonies made absolutely no impression on the clouded minds of the pressmen. Franklin did, however, find a new friend at Watts's in a young man named John Wygate. Like Franklin, Wygate was much better educated than the average printer. He loved to read, and he loved to discuss ideas. The two shared other interests as well. Franklin had always wondered why more people did not enjoy swimming, or had never even tried it. He taught Wygate to swim in only two lessons. A few more lessons made him an expert. Once, on a pleasure cruise down the Thames River through London, Wygate asked Franklin to demonstrate his ability. Franklin stripped off his outer clothes and dived into the water. For nearly four miles, right through the city, he swam beside the boat, "performing on the way many feats of activity, both upon and under water, that surprised and pleased those to whom they were novelties."

News of Franklin's swimming ability got around. Before long Sir William Wyndham, a rich nobleman, offered Franklin a large sum to teach his two sons to swim. Franklin and Wygate talked of making a fortune by opening up a swimming school. They even wondered if they could take a trip through Europe by giving swimming demonstrations and lessons to pay their way.

But such plans were not to be. Thomas Denham, the Quaker merchant who had befriended Franklin on the voyage to England, now came to him with a plan. During his eighteen-month stay in London, Franklin had seen Denham often. He had great respect for the older man. Now Denham told Franklin that he had made his purchases and would soon go back to Philadelphia. Would Franklin return with him? Then help him to open a new store? More than that, Denham was willing to pay part of Franklin's passage back to Philadelphia. Even more, as Franklin got to know the business, he would be given a larger and larger share of it.

Franklin could hardly say no. He quit his job at Watts's. He helped Thomas Denham make a few remaining purchases. Finally, the two men sailed from England on the *Berkshire*, a ship bound for Philadelphia, on July 2, 1726.

The east-to-west trip, Franklin knew, would probably take longer than the voyage to England. Most passengers boarded the ship with frowns on their faces and weeks of boredom already in their minds. But not Ben Franklin. He knew his days in London had come to an end right when they should have. He looked forward to Philadelphia.

Benjamin Franklin at the age of twenty.

When a mind like Franklin's went aboard a ship, it immediately started to ask questions about everything in sight. Soon Franklin was regularly dipping a thermometer into the water, trying to map the path of the Gulf Stream through the Atlantic. He learned that porpoises could be caught with a special kind of bait, a candle with two feathers stuck in it. When the porpoises saw what looked like a flying fish—their favorite kind of food—they snapped at it before it even touched the water. Late one evening Franklin saw a rare sight indeed, "a rainbow in the night, caused by the moon." One day, just as he was about to dive into the sea for a needed bath, he saw a large shark already there, swimming slowly around the ship. All these experiences he recorded in a diary later published as *Journal of a Voyage.*

Franklin's last diary entry was for Tuesday, October 11: "the most joyful day I ever knew." Under a happy sky, the *Berkshire* made its slow way up the Delaware River toward Philadelphia. Franklin set foot in the city at about ten at night. The passengers congratulated each other for "having completed so tedious and dangerous a voyage. Thank God!"

During his last days at sea, Franklin did some other writing, not to be found in the pages of his diary. He realized that he was headed toward a new life. Twenty years of living had given him a lot of experience and knowledge—but so far, he didn't have much to show for it. He had made mistakes, bad mistakes, with people: James Collins, Sir William Keith, James Ralph. Now he must make no more mistakes. As an author plans an essay before he starts to write, so a person should plan his own life before living it. To this end, Franklin wrote down four resolutions he swore to live by:

1. He would watch every penny until he had paid his debts.
2. He would always speak the truth and be sincere.
3. He would work hard and not be led astray by "any foolish project of growing suddenly rich." Hard work and patience were the best way to a fortune.
4. He would speak ill of no one, even if it were the truth.

On October 11, 1726, Ben Franklin had his plan for the future pretty well in mind. Now it was on to a new life.

CHAPTER

6

A New Life

In the days that followed, Ben Franklin learned what had happened in Philadelphia during his stay in London. He was particularly interested in three people: Sir William Keith, Samuel Keimer, and Deborah Read.

Keith, he learned, was no longer governor. In spite of Sir William's faults, he had done a good job for the people of Pennsylvania. Keith had been behind many good laws. But he had not pleased the proprietors, the top-level aristocrats upon whose favor his job depended. Now Sir William lived in Philadelphia as a private citizen. One day Franklin saw him approaching on the street. It must have been an awkward moment for both. They solved the problem by passing in silence.

Samuel Keimer still ran his print shop. He seemed to have a lot of business. Franklin thought this was due to the lack of competition, not to Keimer's ability. In England,

Franklin had heard some stories about Keimer from a woman who had once lived with him as his wife. Now he wanted to have absolutely nothing to do with this "odd fish" of a printer.

News about Deborah Read was sad indeed. Although they had been engaged when Ben sailed off to London, he had written her only one letter. Her reaction was a normal one: In this case, no news was bad news. She had tried to forget Ben. A potter named Rogers asked for her hand in marriage. He was a good worker, and Debby's friends encouraged the match. She agreed—only to find herself miserable. Rogers ran up many debts and was constantly in trouble. Then Debby heard stories about a wife whom he already had in England. She left him. As for Rogers, he then left his troubles by running away to the West Indies. Now there were rumors that Rogers had died. Were they true? Had Deborah ever been a legal wife—and if so, was she still legally married? Nobody was sure. At any rate, Debby now refused to bear his name. Once again she called herself Miss Read.

Franklin threw his energies into Thomas Denham's business. Denham's new store on Water Street was a success. Franklin kept the books and learned to wait on customers in a way that brought success. He and Denham boarded in the same house. They were like father and son. "I respected and loved him," Franklin wrote later. But early in 1727, both men fell ill. Franklin's illness was pleurisy, a disease of the lungs. He suffered greatly. At one point he was near death. Thomas Denham did die. The people in charge of his affairs took over, and the shop was closed. Once again, Franklin was without a job.

And once again, Samuel Keimer entered the picture. The long-bearded printer came to Franklin with a proposal. He was expanding his business to include a stationery shop. But he couldn't be in two places at the same time. He had also assembled half a dozen "raw, cheap hands" to strengthen his printing business. He offered Franklin a generous salary to become his foreman in the print shop.

Franklin was suspicious. It wasn't like Samuel Keimer to pay high wages to anybody. And his workers—an assorted crew that ranged from a farmhand to a newly arrived indentured servant—knew little about printing. Franklin thought that just as soon as he taught the workers what they needed to know, Keimer would dismiss him or lower his pay. Nevertheless, no other job was at hand. He needed the money, as he still expected Vernon's debt to be called for. He said yes.

Franklin's efforts brought steady improvement to Keimer's print shop. Some of the new men he made compositors, some pressmen. One he put to bookbinding. Three of the workers had the special qualities that Franklin looked for in a friend. Young George Webb not long before had been a scholar at Oxford University in England. Thomas Godfrey was a self-taught mathematician, a brilliant man. Hugh Meredith was the thirty-year-old son of a prosperous Pennsylvania farmer. Meredith was "honest, sensible,... something of a reader, but given to drink."

There was steady improvement, too, in Franklin's own education. His new life turned out to be a good one. Self-education, he discovered, need not be self-driven loneliness. He knew other young men who wanted to better themselves. A dozen of these he invited to become members of a new club, the Junto. (The Spanish word *junta* means "discussion group.") The Junto would be an exchange place for friendship, knowledge, and ideas.

Throughout American history, thousands of clubs have been formed by young men on their way up. Not one of them, however, is as well known as Franklin's Junto. Its first members were a cross section of Philadelphia society and business. Only one of them could be called wealthy. Three besides Franklin came from Keimer's shop. The others included a clerk, a shoemaker, a glassworker, a surveyor, and a carpenter. Their common belief was that no man should be limited by his place in life or his occupation.

At first the Junto met in the back room of a tavern on Friday nights. This was a logical place, for Franklin's ritual included a break now and then for a glass of beer or wine. The rest of the ritual began with a reading of twenty-four questions. Some examples:

1. Have you met with anything in the author you last read, remarkable or suitable to be communicated to the Junto...?
2. What new story have you lately heard agreeable for telling in conversation?
3. Hath any citizen in your knowledge failed in his business lately, and what have you heard of the cause?
13. Do you know of any deserving young beginner lately set up, whom it lies in the power of the Junto any way to encourage?
16. Hath anyone attacked your reputation lately? And what can the Junto do toward securing it?

After a break, the Junto turned to the real business of the evening: discussion of an original paper that had been read at the previous session. The members took turns writing these papers, so that everyone had about four chances a year. The papers were supposed to answer a question that had been decided on beforehand. Some of the questions were high-toned indeed: Can a person ever become so good and virtuous as to become perfect, or is this impossible? What really accounts for happiness? What is wisdom? If a government deprives a person of his rights, does he have a right to resist? Other questions were more down-to-earth: What makes some fireplaces smoke? What accounts for the moisture that gathers on a glass of cold water in the summer?

Franklin's rules allowed a week to pass between the reading of a paper and the discussion of it. This gave members time for additional reading and thinking on the subject. Even the discussion itself followed set rules. Members were not allowed to go head-on against one another in argument. Franklin had long known that the way to win an argument was to seem not to argue. No, the person in a dispute should pretend to be humble, even shy. Words like *certainly* and *undoubtedly* should be avoided. Instead, the person should calmly invite the other to join him in a search for truth: "It appears to me..." "I should think it so and so, for such and such reasons." "It is so, if I am not mistaken." Franklin's rules for avoiding heated arguments served him well throughout life. Small wonder that, years later, when the colonists needed a diplomat to send to the capitals of Europe, Benjamin Franklin was exactly the man.

Franklin's Junto was to last for thirty years. Several members, like the founder himself, went on to great success. From the very beginning, they helped each other in every way possible. For instance, all shoe business went to the shoemaker. The men lent each other money from time to time. In fact, the Junto was so successful that the members had to keep it a secret, if only to keep the wrong kind of people from applying. As time passed, Franklin even thought of starting an International Brotherhood of Juntos that would reform the whole human race. But he was always too busy to get the project under way.

Even when the Junto itself was just getting under way, Franklin was busy with other matters. His predictions about Samuel Keimer proved correct. After Franklin had spent about six months on the job, Keimer wanted to cut his wages. Keimer's real reason was clear: The men were now so well trained that, with Keimer's help, they could operate the print shop on their own. Of course, Franklin said no to Keimer's proposal. Then Keimer began to criticize and to pick little quarrels, all in an effort to make Franklin quit.

Finally Keimer was successful. One day Franklin heard some disturbance on the street outside. He stuck his head out the window. Keimer, out on the street, immediately started to yell. Franklin was wasting his time! He should get back to business! Franklin felt the flash fire of anger. Keimer had no good reason to lash him with words before so many people. Keimer entered the shop, and the two exchanged words that not only lashed but stung. Franklin's rage left him no other choice. He quit. Period. Picking up only his hat, he stalked out of the shop.

That evening Hugh Meredith stopped by Franklin's room with the rest of his things from Keimer's. The two got to talking. Meredith had no more use for Keimer than Franklin had. In Meredith's opinion, Keimer was a sloppy man, a poor printer, and no businessman at all. Meredith knew that he was in debt for everything in his shop. His creditors were at his heels. Often he took on jobs for small-but-quick sums of money, just to satisfy one of the dogs at his heels. Surely, Meredith said, Keimer would fail before long. Who in Philadelphia would take his place as a printer? Meredith had an idea. He had already talked the matter over with his father, a successful farmer. His father would set Franklin and him up in business for themselves. In other words, the partnership would start with Meredith cash and Franklin skill. The two would divide the profits equally.

Franklin liked the plan. He talked it over with Hugh Meredith's father. The farmer seemed more than sincere. Franklin was pretty sure that beneath the surface, Mr. Meredith had another aim. Only too well did the older man know his son's taste for alcohol. He also knew that Franklin had helped his son try to overcome the habit. Ben Franklin was a good influence. If the two young men became partners, his son might become both sober and successful. At any rate, Franklin gave Hugh's father a list of all the equipment the new print shop would need. This was sent for at once. Hugh Meredith kept on working for Keimer, bubbling on the inside with his secret plans.

Not long after, Franklin received an unexpected letter from Samuel Keimer. Old friends should not part because of a senseless quarrel, Keimer stated. Anyone can get angry; anyone can forgive and be forgiven. Franklin went on reading. It seemed that Keimer had the chance to print the new paper money for the colony of New Jersey. Franklin knew that this would involve copperplate printing and someone who could cut the designs for the bills. Clearly, Keimer had to have Franklin's skills if he was to do the job at all. The pay was excellent. So once again, for still another time, Benjamin Franklin went to work for Samuel Keimer.

The printing of money was very official business. It had to be done under close supervision at Burlington, New

Franklin was an industrious worker and a shrewd businessman.

Jersey. Keimer and Franklin spent nearly three months on the job. During that time, Franklin was invited into the homes of several important people. He carefully formed friendships with people who could do him good in the future.

The printing equipment from London arrived right after the New Jersey job ended. Franklin and Meredith quit Keimer's employ. They rented a house with a shop and hung out a sign. Their first job came from an old country-man whom a friend had found wandering around Philadelphia in search of a printer.

The rented house had more space than Franklin and Meredith needed. To save expenses, they rented the extra rooms to the family of Thomas Godfrey, a fellow Junto member. Godfrey, a self-educated mathematical wizard, earned his living as a glassworker. There was room on the street for Godfrey to open a shop of his own. Franklin and Hugh Meredith could eat their meals at the Godfrey table.

To succeed in business, Franklin knew he would have to work harder than he had ever worked in his life. He again resolved to be truthful and upright in all dealings. He tried to produce quality printing at a good price. In general, he was the compositor, Meredith the pressman. So many things can go wrong in printing that to keep up with orders, Franklin often stayed up late at night. He was careful, too, to appear just as industrious as he was. For instance, when a load of paper needed to be brought through the streets to the shop, he would go out and push the wheelbarrow himself, just to be seen. "The industry of that Franklin," one wealthy merchant remarked to some friends, "is superior to anything I ever saw of the kind; I see him still at work when I go home from the club, and he is at work again before his neighbors are out of bed."

As a businessman, there is no doubt that Franklin was an upright man, and honest in keeping his promises to himself. But he was also quick to seize upon any opportunity that came along. For instance, soon after setting up shop—and certainly remembering his days in Boston—he thought of starting a newspaper. The only paper in Philadelphia was Andrew Bradford's *American Weekly Mercury*, which Franklin thought dull. However, Samuel Keimer heard of Franklin's plans. Keimer, who was constantly trying to expand a business always on the verge of collapse, rushed a newspaper of his own into print. Now Franklin would have two competitors, not one. Franklin carefully put together his plan of attack. Remembering his old days alias SILENCE DOGOOD, he sent a stream of clever, amusing pieces off to Bradford's paper. Bradford was happy to print them. They proved popular. Bradford's circulation went up, Keimer's down. Before long Keimer was reduced to ninety subscribers. Needing money as usual, Keimer was willing to sell *The Pennsylvania Gazette* to Franklin for a small sum.

Under Franklin's management, the *Gazette* soon became the leading newspaper—not only in Pennsylvania, but in all the colonies. As for Samuel Keimer, he was soon forced to give up the printing battle in Philadelphia. Deeply in debt, he moved to Barbados, an island in the West Indies.

Even when no opportunity came along, Franklin created an opportunity. For several years, Andrew Bradford had been the official printer for Pennsylvania. This meant that he printed copies of laws, important speeches, regulations—all the printing the government required. One day there fell into Franklin's hands a copy of an address the Pennsylvania Assembly (the colony's legislature) had prepared for the governor. Bradford, of course, had printed it. Franklin thought the printing shoddy and careless. "We printed it elegantly and correctly," Franklin later wrote, "and sent one to every member." The next year Franklin and Meredith, not Bradford, did Pennsylvania's official printing. Before long Franklin secured Delaware's business also, as well as the printing of that colony's paper money.

Benjamin Franklin's printing press.

As business expanded, the main threat to Franklin came from inside the partnership, not from the outside. The firm slowly became more and more Franklin, less and less Meredith. By 1729, Meredith, according to Franklin "was often seen drunk in the streets." Instead of doing his share of the work, Hugh Meredith was gambling away his afternoons in taverns. Also, Meredith's father had not yet paid all the bills for the printing equipment. His supplier threatened to sue for the rest of the money. The situation grew dangerous.

At this point, two Junto members, William Coleman and Robert Grace, came to Franklin independently. Each said he would be glad to let Franklin have whatever loan was needed to get through the crisis. Franklin then had a showdown with Hugh Meredith. It was really no contest. "I see this is a business I was not fit for," Meredith said. "I was bred a farmer, and it was folly for me to come to town, and put myself, at thirty years of age, an apprentice to learn a new trade." In short, Meredith wanted to return to the plow. He was more than willing to let Franklin buy him out for thirty pounds and the firm's debts. Franklin borrowed half the money from Coleman, half from Grace. He had taken on debts, but he also had sole control of the business that would pay them off.

Franklin was now twenty-four. He ran his own print shop and even employed others. His debts were not as dark as his prospects were bright. Keimer had been disposed of, and another rival, David Henry, had also gone out of business. At last Franklin had the luxury to turn to another interest: marriage.

Franklin approached the subject in his own practical way. He still boarded with the Godfrey family. Mrs. Godfrey, knowing that Franklin was a good catch, set herself up as matchmaker. One day she invited an attractive young relative to dinner. The invitation was extended again, again, and again. Whenever possible, the Godfreys left the young couple alone. Before long Franklin told the Godfreys that yes, certainly, he was willing—if only the dowry was large enough to pay off his debts. (A common practice at the time, a dowry was a gift from the bride's parents to get a marriage under way.) Franklin wanted a hundred pounds. Mrs. Godfrey negotiated. No, she finally learned. A hundred pounds was out of the question. What future did a printer have? Keimer had failed in the business. David Henry had also gone under. Franklin would probably be next.

Franklin knew that he was headed toward success, not failure. He suspected a trick. Probably, he thought, the young woman's parents thought they would marry for love in any case. Then the matter of a dowry would not be on the negotiating table. This Franklin resented. He told Mrs. Godfrey that he would have nothing more to do with the girl or her family. In a huff, the Godfreys moved out of Franklin's house. The romance was over.

A few other marriage possibilities also came to nothing. Finally, Franklin turned his attention to his flame of six years before, Deborah Read. Debby's short marriage to the potter Rogers had left her sad and solitary. In part, Franklin blamed himself. After all, he had been engaged to Debby. He should have written her regular letters from London and come back as soon as possible. But that wasn't right, said Debby's mother. It wasn't Ben's fault. It was she who had ruled against a marriage until Ben returned.

"Our mutual affection was revived," Franklin wrote later about Debby, "but there were now great objections to our union." Was Debby still legally married to the scoun-

An engraving of Deborah Franklin.

drel Rogers, or not? If so, she could not take a second husband. And even if Rogers were dead, by marrying Debby, Franklin might make himself responsible for Rogers's many debts. The problem was solved in a traditional and simple way: Debby simply moved into Ben's house, and the two declared that they were husband and wife.

The common-law marriage between Benjamin Franklin and Deborah Read (Rogers) has puzzled historians for years. Throughout his life, Franklin had an amazing ability to charm other people, women included. In the Philadelphia of 1730, there must have been hundreds of other eligible young women. Debby was in no way Ben's equal in ability or ambition. Although Ben was to praise her repeatedly, this might simply illustrate his vow to say nothing bad about any person. Others said that Deborah was plump and plain at the best, sharp-tongued and unpleasant at the worst. Ben's *Autobiography* is of little help in this regard. If we take Franklin at his word, he married Debby out of guilt and pity, as much as out of love. Yet throughout a long marriage, he wrote years later, "She proved a good and faithful helpmate.... We throve together, and have ever mutually endeavored to make each other happy."

There is more to the mystery surrounding Franklin's marriage. Soon after their union, the young couple took into their home an infant, the illegitimate son of Benjamin Franklin. Who was the child's mother? Why didn't—or couldn't—Ben marry her? Was the baby a part of the common-law marriage agreement that Ben proposed and Debby accepted? These questions have never been answered. All we know is that Ben raised little William as his beloved son. That is surely to his credit.

7

"The Way to Wealth"

Ben Franklin's fling at romance and marriage was hardly a detour in his business career. In fact, it was not even a brief stop. The Godfrey family, having failed as matchmakers, had now moved out of Ben's house. This left vacant the shop that Thomas Godfrey had used for his glass business. With Debby's able hands to help him, Ben had found a partnership that would prosper.

What started as a stationery store soon expanded to other lines. The shop began selling books as well. Then came chocolate, coffee, wine, and powdered mustard. From a brother in Rhode Island came scented soap, fancy cheese, and dried codfish. A buyer as well as a seller, Franklin built up quite a business taking in old linen rags for resale to paper mills. The ads in his *Gazette* offered occasional lots of lumber and barrels of fish. There seems to have been almost nothing that Franklin would not buy, sell, or trade for a small profit.

Although later in life Franklin was to join the antislavery movement, as a young merchant he traded in slaves along with everything else. These he advertised in the *Gazette:* "A likely Negro wench about fifteen years old, has had the smallpox, been in the country above a year and talks English. Inquire of the printer hereof." From time to time, Ben and Debby used slaves for personal service in the house. But even as a young man, Franklin saw no future for slavery. For one thing, it was poor business. All costs considered, he wrote, wage labor was cheaper than slave labor, at least in the northern colonies. And for another, slaves in a household had a bad effect on the owners' children: "The white children become proud, disgusted with labor, and being educated in idleness, are rendered unfit to get a living by industry [hard work]."

No, for Franklin nothing could get in the way of his two favorite words, *industry* and *frugality* [saving money]. And in these matters, few people could equal his wife, Debby. "She assisted me cheerfully in my business," he wrote later, "folding and stitching pamphlets, tending shop, purchasing old linen rags for the paper makers, etc., etc. We kept no idle servants, our table [diet] was plain and simple, our furniture of the cheapest."

Wherever he looked, Franklin seemed to find another way to wealth. Shortly before his marriage, he had written a pamphlet that called on the Pennsylvania Assembly for an issue of paper money. Commerce was slow, he noted. Increase the money supply, and business would boom. When the Assembly finally acted on his suggestion, Franklin was overjoyed—especially as he got the job of printing the bills. About this time, too, Franklin found that he had enough cash to set another printer up in business. Thomas Whitemarsh, one of his trusted workers, was sent off to

Charleston, South Carolina, there to open a shop with Franklin as a silent partner. In return for the start-up expenses, Ben was to get a third of the profits. The idea proved a good one. As Franklin trained other printers and heard of places where a shop was needed, he repeated the procedure again and again. Before long a steady stream of profits was rolling in from as far away as the West Indies.

Meanwhile, the Junto continued to meet on Friday nights. Before long the group abandoned the tavern for a room in the house of a member. This had several advantages. One was that the books of all could be brought together to form an informal library, from which anyone could borrow. Then Franklin expanded the idea. Why not form a subscription library that anyone in Philadelphia could join? A lawyer was consulted, and soon subscriptions were offered to the public at large: forty shillings to start, and then ten shillings a year. The first fifty book lovers were hard to find, but at last in 1731 the small Library Company had enough money to send to England for books. Then more and more people joined, and the collection grew ever larger. This, the first subscription library in America, eventually in 1742 became the public library of Philadelphia.

Other good ideas grew out of Junto meetings. Were the streets dangerous at night? Soon night watchmen were being paid for by property owners. Was the downtown section poorly lighted? Franklin again had a proposal, and again it was accepted, first by the Junto, then by the government. Did fires too often rage out of control? Franklin remembered his days in Boston, where more of the houses were built of wood. The Boston fire companies had done a good job. Now in Philadelphia the Union Fire Company became the city's first.

The year 1732 stands out in Franklin's life for at least three reasons. First, he finally managed to end his life as a debtor; he could even pay off Mr. Vernon, who after years of silence finally asked for his money. Second, Debby gave birth to a boy, Francis Folger Franklin. Called Franky by his loving father, the child was adored by both parents. Debby had never completely accepted William as a son; now she and Ben had their own little boy. And third, on December 19, the first issue of *Poor Richard's Almanack* went on sale.

In eighteenth-century America, there were several things an ambitious printer could do to increase business. For instance, he could publish a weekly newspaper. This Franklin had done since 1729 with *The Pennsylvania Gazette*. Also, he could sell stationery items: paper, ink, ink powders, pens and replacement quills, sealing wax, and the like. Franklin started his busy store by selling such things. Finally, if the printer was truly ambitious, he could start an almanac.

Almanacs were hugely popular in colonial days. After the Holy Bible, the annual almanac was the publication most likely to be found in a home. Farmers planted their crops according to the phases of the moon, and as these changed every year, an almanac was necessary. Almanac calendars also offered weather predictions and all kinds of astrological lore. Other useful information included distances between cities, as well as the best roads and places to stay. Travelers also had to know the rates of exchange between the kinds of money used in different colonies. Almanacs also listed the dates of court sessions and fairs. Many almanacs also included recipes, short poems, and jokes.

Franklin knew that if he could publish a popular

almanac, his market would stretch from New Hampshire to Georgia. He also knew that there was a lot of competition. His would have to be an almanac *with a difference*. Probably, remembering his old days as Silence Dogood, he wanted to start writing for fun again. At any rate, the difference was this: The almanac would appear to be written by an interesting character named Richard Saunders. Franklin could hide behind his invented author and have all the fun he wanted.

POOR RICHARD'S ALMANACK read the cover of the first edition, for 1733. On the title page, Richard Saunders was listed as the author. Only on the bottom of the page, in much smaller type, was it noted that the almanac was "printed and sold by B. Franklin" of Philadelphia.

The introduction to the 1733 edition is a masterpiece. Saunders introduces himself as a shiftless stargazer. The impractical astrologer is married to a most practical woman, who now insists that he finally earn some money. If he doesn't, Saunders says, his wife threatens to burn his books and scientific instruments. Hence the first issue of *Poor Richard's Almanack*.

Saunders goes on to say that in truth, he has wanted to publish an almanac for a long time. He has held back only because of "my regard for my good friend and fellow student Mr. Titan Leeds, whose interest I was extremely unwilling to hurt." Now, in actual fact, Titan Leeds was a real person. For several years Leeds had written an almanac of his own, printed by Andrew Bradford in Philadelphia. But sadly, Saunders goes on to say, Titan Leeds is about to die. The stars and the planets leave no doubt about it. "Death, who was never known to respect merit, has already prepared the mortal dart, the fatal Sister has already extended her destroying shears, and that ingenious man must soon

Poor Richard, 1733.

A N

Almanack

For the Year of Chrift

1733,

Being the Firft after LEAP YEAR:

And makes fince the Creation	Years
By the Account of the Eaftern *Greeks*	7241
By the Latin Church, when ☉ ent. ♈	6932
By the Computation of *W. W*	5742
By the *Roman* CHronology	5682
By the *Jewifh* Rabbies	5494

Wherein is contained

The Lunations, Eclipfes, Judgment of the Weather, Spring Tides, Planets Motions & mutual Afpects, Sun and Moon's Rifing and Setting, Length of Days, Time of High Water, Fairs, Courts, and obfervable Days

Fitted to the Latitude of Forty Degrees, and a Meridian of Five Hours Weft from *London,* but may without fenfible Error, ferve all the adjacent Places, even from *Newfoundland* to *South-Carolina.*

By *RICHARD SAUNDERS,* Philom.

PHILADELPHIA:
Printed and fold by *B. FRANKLIN,* at the New Printing Office near the Market.

The Third Impreffion.

The title page of Poor Richard's Almanack *for 1733.*

be taken from us. He dies, by my calculation made at his request, on Oct. 17, 1733,"—at exactly 3:29 P.M. According to Poor Richard, Leeds's own calculation puts the date at October 26. But the difference is a small one. As to which astrologer is right, only time will tell. But anyhow, Richard Saunders can now launch an almanac with no offense to his esteemed friend Titan Leeds.

Thus Franklin had fun himself while making fun of his chief competitor. Titan Leeds could only strike back in his almanac for the next year. He denounced Richard Saunders in words meant to wound. Leeds pronounced himself still very much alive. And he hoped to "live to write when his [rival's] performances are dead."

It would have been better if Leeds had said nothing, for he only opened the door to more of Franklin's frolicking words. In his own 1734 almanac, Saunders continues the battle. He cannot be sure, he says, whether his friend Titan Leeds died on October 17 or 26. In fact, he cannot be absolutely certain that Leeds has in fact died. Unfortunately, a sickness in his own family

would not permit me as I had intended, to be with him in his last moments, to receive his last embrace, to close his eyes, and do the duty of a friend performing the last offices to the departed.... There is however, (and I cannot speak it without sorrow) there is the strongest probability that my dear friend is no more; for there appears in his name, as I am assured, an almanac for the year 1734, in which I am treated in a very gross and unhandsome manner; in which I am called *a false predictor,* an *ignorant,* a *conceited scribbler,* a *fool* and a *liar.* Mr. Leeds was too well bred to use any man so indecently, and moreover his esteem and affection for me was extraordinary.

In other words, Leeds must be dead, for he was too fine a man to attack an old friend. Therefore, the almanac now published in his name must be written by a scoundrel who thinks he can make some fast money by using Leeds's name. This, Saunders adds, is "an unpardonable injury to his memory, and an imposition upon the public."

So far as is known, Leeds chose not to respond to this second attack. This was probably a wise decision. Franklin could not only write circles around Leeds, he could write verbal hoops that Leeds had to jump through. Leeds's quill pen was no match for Franklin's. The next year, in the 1735 almanac, Franklin has Saunders say that he is now certain that Titan Leeds is dead. The almanac now published in his name is so, so boring. There is no way a man of Leeds's wit, skill, and learning could have written it.

If the Titan Leeds matter got Franklin's almanac off to a flying start, it was Poor Richard's sayings that kept it aloft. Over the years, to fill little spaces on the pages, Franklin inserted hundreds of proverbs. Although these are now often reprinted in Franklin's name, few were original with the author. This he freely admitted; the sayings "contained the wisdom of many ages and nations." In the 1730s, Franklin taught himself to read French, Italian, Spanish, and German. He could search the literature of Europe for "scraps from the table of wisdom." Franklin's achievement was first to find these proverbs, then to put his special verbal spin on them, so that they struck home true. For instance, there is an old English saying, "A muffled cat is no good mouser." Franklin's version has sharper claws: "A cat in gloves catches no mice."

Many of Poor Richard's sayings concern Franklin's two top virtues, industry and frugality:

Early to bed and early to rise makes a man healthy, wealthy and wise.

Keep thy shop, and thy shop will keep thee.

God helps them that help themselves.

A thrifty maxim of the wary Dutch, is to save all the money they can touch.

Other proverbs cover many aspects of life. Often they make the reader think twice:

Keep your eyes wide open before marriage, half shut afterwards.

Fish and visitors smell in three days.

Where there's marriage without love there will be love without marriage.

A countryman between two lawyers is like a fish between two cats.

Make haste slowly.

Franklin kept *Poor Richard's Almanack* going for years, long after he had retired from active life as a printer. Over ten thousand copies a year made him a good profit. Much later, in 1757, he found some free time while sailing to London on a ship. He was by then a diplomat, and he knew that the next *Poor Richard* would be his last. He sat down with twenty-five years' worth of sayings in front of him, intending to make a list of the best.

But Franklin wasn't content to make a simple list. No, he had to think of an interesting way to present the proverbs. He started writing a story. An old man called Father Abraham rises to speak to a crowd at a country fair. Are the people angry about ever-rising taxes? Well, says the ancient wise man, taxes laid on by the government are nothing compared with taxes people lay on themselves— through lack of *industry* and *frugality*. Father Abraham works an old saying into his speech, then another and another and another.

Father Abraham's speech goes on for pages. Soon it was printed separately as *The Way to Wealth*. Then it was translated into French, German, Spanish, Polish, Russian, Chinese, and other languages. The name Benjamin Franklin became known around the world.

Franklin had no sooner got the almanac under way than he turned to another well-known aspect of his life. This was the search for personal perfection. One of his Junto papers had asked the question: Can a person be so good and virtuous as to be perfect, or is this impossible? In 1733 he decided to use his own life as an experiment. He was determined to find out.

In his *Autobiography*, Franklin describes the experiment in great detail. First he wrote down a list of twelve virtues, with short rules for each. He started with *temperance*: "Eat not to dullness; drink not to elevation." To this he added *silence*: "Speak not but what may benefit others or yourself; avoid trifling conversation." Then came *order, resolution, frugality, industry, sincerity, justice, moderation, cleanliness, tranquility* [calmness], and *chastity*. As an afterthought, he added *humility*, or freedom from pride.

His list complete, Franklin ruled off some notebook pages with red ink. On the left he listed the virtues. On the top were the days of the week. His plan was to review each day in the evening. He would make a little black spot in the grid pattern for every failing. But this proved too much to undertake at one time. Instead, he devoted a week to temperance alone. When he felt he had mastered that virtue, he went on to the next. The thirteen virtues took him thirteen weeks. "I could go through a course complete in thirteen weeks, and four courses a year. . . . After a while I went through one course only in a year, and afterward only one in several years." By that time, Franklin had found some sheets of ivory for his notebook. He could simply wipe the penciled spots off with a sponge, instead of having to rule off more paper. Eventually, Franklin dropped the practice. But he always kept the little note-book with him, to the end of his days. As an old man, humility did not prevent him from showing it to others with some pride.

Did the experiment succeed? No, Franklin himself admitted. The perfect human being is probably a contra-diction in terms. "But on the whole," he wrote years later, "though I never arrived at the perfection I had been so ambitious of obtaining, but fell far short of it, yet I was, by the endeavor [attempt], a better and happier man than I should otherwise have been."

Along with Franklin's attempt at perfection came another attempt to find exactly where he stood with regard to religion. Once, in England, he had written a pamphlet expressing his doubts. Now he had seen what happened to people who did not take religion seriously. His onetime friends Collins and Ralph were good examples. Lack of religion had resulted in personal failings. Franklin now decided that he did very much believe in God, though it was hard for him to attend church regularly. He wrote out long and short versions of a personal prayer. He believed that leading a useful life was a better way to honor God than the public display of worship.

This period in Franklin's life was generally a successful one. In 1736 he was made clerk of the Pennsylvania Assembly. The work itself was tiresome, but it brought him into contact with the kind of people it paid—really *paid*—to know. The next year he was made postmaster of Philadelphia. This too had its advantages: Now he could send his *Gazette* to subscribers without having to bribe the mail riders. Yet there were disappointments as well. Because there were many German settlers in Pennsylvania, Franklin purchased some German type and put out a newspaper in that language. It failed after a few issues. A magazine for which he had high hopes also had to be dropped as a money loser.

Franklin's main disappointment was certainly the death of his son. His beloved little Franky died of smallpox in 1736, at four years of age. Franklin's sadness lasted as long as he lived. At the time the able young man felt absolutely helpless. He could only have Franky's portrait painted from memory and write the heartfelt words for his tombstone: "The DELIGHT of all that knew him."

In 1743 a daughter, Sarah, was born and took a place in her parents' hearts. Franklin called her Sally and loved her dearly, but she never quite filled the vacant space in her father's soul. Or maybe Franklin never really gave her a chance. At that time he was busier than ever. He was making arrangements to have an excellent printer, David Hall, come from England to join his still-growing printing business.

David Hall turned out to be everything Franklin hoped for in a printer. More and more, Franklin found it possible to let Hall run the shop, while he turned to other interests. By 1748 Hall was ready to take over the whole operation. At the age of forty-two, Franklin found that he had enough money to retire. Even though he would take no active part in the business, it would still pay him nearly a thousand pounds a year. An equal amount would come from other sources: his part-time positions as postmaster and Assembly clerk, as well as rents on houses he owned and money from silent partnerships.

Two thousand pounds a year was a lot of money. It was more than the salary of the governor of Pennsylvania. Franklin bought a three-hundred-acre farm in New Jersey. He also moved to a bigger and more comfortable house in Philadelphia. Part of the year, he thought, he would be a country gentleman. The rest of the time he would spend in the city—as a member of the leisure class.

CHAPTER

8

Lightning from the Skies

Benjamin Franklin was to spend little time on his New Jersey farm. For him a life of leisure did not mean a life of idleness. No, leisure time was time that could be put to uses other than running a business or making money. Franklin's nimble brain had long been drawn to science and invention. When he "retired" in 1748, he knew that some surprises lay just around a corner in his mind.

For years, Franklin's *Gazette* had tried to keep its readers up to date with natural philosophy, as science was then called. The Junto had also tried to keep up with what was happening. Out of a Junto discussion in 1743 had come Franklin's *Proposal for Promoting Useful Knowledge*. This pamphlet urged colonists with scientific interests to correspond with each other. Franklin sent copies to everyone he thought might be interested. He called for an organization that would promote the exchange of knowledge. Out of Franklin's proposal in 1743 came the American Philosophical Society, the first scientific organization in America.

During the early 1740s, too, Franklin perfected what he called the "Pennsylvanian Fireplace." Nowadays people talk about Franklin stoves, meaning any shallow, upright stove with an open front for viewing the fire. But Franklin's own invention was far superior to what passes for a Franklin stove today. His excitement about the invention bubbled over into a long pamphlet on the subject, *An Account of the New Invented Pennsylvanian Fireplaces* (1744).

We are living in the modern age, Franklin tells his readers. The days when huge forests surrounded American cities are gone. Now wood has to be hauled as much as a hundred miles to heat our homes. This means that the days of the wood-guzzling fireplace are gone. A properly designed stove can produce twice as much heat with a quarter the wood. The trouble with fireplaces is that they let nearly all the heat rush up the chimney. Roaring fires need air to burn, and where does this air come from? From outside the room to be heated, of course. The larger the blaze in the fireplace, the more cold air is drawn into the room through cracks around windows and doors. "In short, it is next to impossible to warm a room with such a fireplace; and I suppose our ancestors never thought of warming rooms to sit in; all they proposed was to have a place to make a fire in, by which they might warm themselves when cold."

Franklin's stove was a cast-iron affair, made of sections that could be taken apart easily for cleaning. The whole thing was held together by two vertical rods, really long bolts, on either side. The stove had no legs but squatted solidly on the hearth of an old fireplace. Air to feed the fire entered the stove through a passageway in the hearth that led to the cellar or outside. This meant that the stove did not constantly pull cold air into the far reaches of the room to be heated.

The stove had another advantage as well. Air from the lower passage also entered an iron warming box immediately in back of the fire. Baffles inside this box made this air circulate back and forth until it emerged as heat from holes high in the sides. Because warm air rises, this provided a constant circulation of heated air into the room.

Franklin turned production of the stove over to his friend Robert Grace. It was Grace who had lent Franklin money to buy out Meredith, and the fellow Junto member had since refused payment on the loan. Grace manufactured the stove and sold many throughout the colonies. Franklin, however, refused to patent his invention, even when told a patent was his for the asking. (To take out a patent means to register an idea and design with the government. A patent is a government document giving the inventor rights to the invention for a limited time. A patent gives the inventor the right to prevent others from making, using, or selling the invention.) Ben Franklin believed that useful inventions should contribute to the public good, not to the bank account of the inventor. As a result, anyone could make and sell the Pennsylvanian Fireplace. Grace failed to make a fortune, but fewer colonists shivered through the long, cold winters.

It was fire from the skies, however, not fire on the hearth, that blazed Franklin's fame around the world. Even today, when most people hear Franklin's name, they probably don't think of the Junto, the almanac, the American Philosophical Society, the University of Pennsylvania (the forerunner of which he also helped found in 1751), the

The Franklin stove, known as the Pennsylvanian Fireplace.

Declaration of Independence, or even the Constitution of the United States. No, the name Benjamin Franklin means first of all the man who flew the kite in the thunderstorm.

Franklin's interest in electricity started even before he left the printing business. In 1743, on a visit to Boston, he attended some lectures given by an English doctor and amateur scientist, Archibald Spencer. Some of Dr. Spencer's demonstrations involved electricity, a new subject to Franklin. Although Ben Franklin later said that the demonstrations were "imperfectly performed," he could not forget them.

One of Franklin's English contacts at the time was a wealthy businessman and part-time scientist named Peter Collinson. It was Collinson who had handled the London end of the Library Company's business from the very beginning. Franklin had struck up a lively correspondence with this man so much like himself. In 1745 Collinson sent the Library Company a pamphlet on electricity and a huge glass rod. When the rod was rubbed with fabric, it would produce the long popping sparks that Ben Franklin had seen in Archibald Spencer's demonstrations. Before long Franklin had repeated all the electrical experiments so far known. He had even started to think about new ones.

In the 1740s, electrical demonstrations were the latest fad in England and the rest of Europe. Franklin had seen Dr. Spencer suspend a boy in the air on silk cords, then make the boy's hair stand on end and sparks fly from his ears. Other tricks included an electrified fly and spider. When the spider got too close to the fly—ZAP, the usual happened. In France, for the amusement of King Louis XV, a scientist had connected 180 soldiers together with iron wire. A sudden electrical shock made all of them jump into the air at the same time. The demonstration was later repeated with a 900-foot-long row of 700 monks in a monastery.

But Franklin's interest in electricity went beyond jumping spiders and monks. He was more interested in the *why* and the *what*. Fortunately, he had at his disposal two recent inventions. The first was the Leyden jar, a device for storing an electric charge. Invented in Holland in 1745, the Leyden jar was a wide-mouthed glass bottle. Inside and outside, the jar was coated on the bottom and partway up the sides with metal foil. Through a hole in a cork or wooden stopper, a metal rod passed into the jar and made contact with the inner foil through water or loose shot. On top of the rod was a small metal ball. Electricity fed to the inside of the jar would be stored there because the glass insulated it from the outer foil. When a wire or chain connected to the outer foil was drawn near the ball—ZIPPITY ZAP, a huge spark. The jolt from a good-sized Leyden jar was enough to kill a chicken.

Electricity to charge the jar came from what was called an *electrical machine*. Today, we would call it a crude *generator*. This was a simple device that saved people the labor of endlessly rubbing large rods with fabric or fur. Franklin's improved electrical machine is still on display at the Franklin Institute in Philadelphia. A glass ball is geared to a rotating handle so that it can be made to spin rapidly. The ball rubs against a leather pad. Touching it also are four metal needles that draw off the electric charge for storage in a Leyden jar.

In Franklin's day, electricity was a little-understood marvel. It was commonly called a *fluid*. Franklin used this word, as well as *fire* and *force*. It was also thought that this fluid came in two kinds. One was called *vitreous* electricity, produced by rubbing a glass rod with fabric. The other was *resinous* electricity, produced by rubbing a rod of amber or hard rubber.

Franklin's first great discovery was that there are not two kinds of electricity but one—or, rather, that the two "kinds" are two aspects of the same thing. He noted that when a man with a vitreous charge stood on an insulating wax mat and touched a person in contact with the ground, a spark preceded the actual touch. The same thing happened when another man on a wax mat had a resinous charge. But if the men on the mats tried to touch each other, a much larger spark flew between the two. Lacking words for what he wanted to explain, Franklin had to invent them. The man on the ground, he said, was electrified in the normal way, or neutral. The vitreous charge

Franklin's device to generate electricity.

Franklin called *positive,* the resinous charge *negative:* Positive and negative, opposites yes, but the *plus* and *minus* aspects of a single force, electricity. This was Franklin's *single-fluid theory* of electricity. It led to rapid progress in the field.

As he continued to experiment, Franklin was forced to invent more new terms for what he wanted to describe. In addition to *positive (plus)* and *negative (minus),* Franklin was the first to use *battery, conductor, armature, brush,* and over ten other electrical terms now in common use.

Franklin's equipment, by our standards, was crude indeed. It looked like what a budget-strapped junior-high teacher might today put together for classroom use. For instance, one key experiment was simply this: Franklin placed a heavy iron ball on top of a bottle, which insulated it enough to retain an electric charge. Then from the ceiling he suspended a smaller cork ball on an insulating silk string. The point of suspension was right above the iron ball, so that the cork ball hung against the side of the iron ball. When the iron ball was charged with electricity, it repelled the cork ball, which swung out several inches from the iron. Then Franklin moved a very large metal needle toward the iron ball. When the point of the needle advanced to about seven inches from the iron ball, the cork ball returned to hang against the iron. Somehow the sharp point of the needle had drawn off the charge. Then he did the same thing, but this time using a rod with a blunt end instead of a needle point. The rod had to move to an inch of the iron ball before the charge decreased. It seemed clear that a grounded sharp metal point could draw electricity through the air. This Franklin called the *doctrine of points.* It led directly to the lightning rod, a most practical invention. Franklin's lightning rod was a sharp metal point that attracted electricity from storm clouds and fed it harmlessly into the ground.

But first Franklin had to prove that lightning and electricity were, in fact, the same thing. Since 1746, he had been reporting his experiments in letters to Peter Collinson. In 1750, he wrote Collinson that the lightning experiment could be easily made. A tall, sharply pointed rod mounted on a high building, he said, should draw enough electricity from storm clouds to be tested. He described the experiment in detail. The next year, Collinson published all of Franklin's writings on electricity in a pamphlet, *Experiments and Observations on Electricity.* The pamphlet was translated into French and other languages. In May 1752, a Frenchman named Dalibard performed Franklin's experiment—successfully! During a tremendous thunderstorm, Dalibard proved that what was called lightning in the sky became electricity when captured for experiments on the ground.

Meanwhile, Franklin himself had not tried the experiment. He was probably waiting for the completion of a Philadelphia church that would tower over all other buildings. Then, in the spring of 1752, he was hit by a bolt of mental lightning: Why not use a kite? One day in June, a month after Dalibard's experiment but before Franklin had heard of it, the weather looked just right. Franklin decided to give his kite idea a try. He and his son hurried to a large, open field that had a shed on one side of it.

Much of the information that has come down to us about the kite experiment is really misinformation. Some accounts have the key attached to the kite itself. Wrong. Some pictures show lightning forking through the sky. Wrong again. Franklin would never have risked his life to a lightning bolt. Other pictures show his son, William, who helped him, as a small boy. In truth, William was in his early twenties at the time. What really happened was this:

The kite, made of silk instead of paper to withstand wind and rain, had a sharply pointed wire extending about a foot from its top. The wire was connected to the kite string, and the string, near the ground, to a key. Franklin reasoned that when the string got damp, the electrical charge in a dark cloud overhead would be attracted by the metal point and conducted down to the key. If that happened, when he reached out his knuckle toward the key, there should be a spark.

Two safety precautions were involved. First, a short length of silk ribbon was attached to the key. Franklin controlled the kite by the other end of the silk ribbon, not by the kite string itself. Silk, he knew, was a good insulator, and it would not absorb water as would the kite string. If a dangerous charge did come down the string, the silk would prevent it from reaching his body. Also, while the kite was going up, Franklin moved to the protection of an open shed. Thus there was no way the silk could get wet.

Soon the kite was aloft, and the right kind of dark cloud was overhead. At first nothing happened. Then, even before it started to rain, Franklin noticed that the small fibers on the kite string were straining outward. He knew from experience what this meant: The string was electrified. The dampness in the air was enough to make the string conduct electricity. He reached out his knuckle toward the key—and history was made. Later the charge was transferred from the key to a Leyden jar. The "lightning from the skies" proved to be perfectly ordinary electricity.

Many experts since that time have pointed out what Franklin did not know: just how dangerous this experi-

William (left) *and Benjamin Franklin conducting the famous electricity experiment. This engraving shows Benjamin reaching toward the key with his knuckles as he holds a Leyden jar. The artist represents William as being much younger than he was at the time of the experiment.*

ment was. The charge in the key came from atmospheric electricity alone. If lightning had suddenly struck a kite held by a wet string, Franklin's life might have been over at that instant—and at age forty-six. In fact, not long afterward, a scientist in Russia did meet his death trying to perform Franklin's lightning experiment.

Franklin never received the shock of his death, but the shock of his life is another story. He experimented with putting chickens to death with Leyden-jar suddenness. The meat tasted better, he thought, "uncommonly tender." Then he wondered, what about a turkey? With some friends on hand to observe the event, he hooked up two huge Leyden jars and charged them to the limit. They packed the power of forty ordinary Leyden jars. As Franklin chatted with his friends, his mind was not fully on the job. He reached out to test one of the "inner" wires, to see if the jars were fully charged—forgetting that he was holding the "outer" chain in the other hand. "The flash was very great and the crack as loud as a pistol," said his friends. Franklin neither saw nor heard anything. He was knocked out of his senses by the "universal blow through my whole body from head to foot which seemed within as well as without." The hand that had held the chain turned a ghastly white and felt like "dead flesh." Slowly he recovered, but two days later he still felt a soreness in his chest.

History does not record what then happened to the turkey.

As Benjamin Franklin's work continued, Peter Collinson continued to publish longer editions of Franklin's *Experiments and Observations on Electricity.* In 1753 both Harvard University and Yale University awarded Franklin the honorary degree of master of arts. *Experiments and Observations* was translated into many languages and was soon joined by the same author's *The Way to Wealth.* In 1759 Franklin was given an honorary doctor's degree by the University of St. Andrews in Scotland. From then on he was commonly called "Dr. Franklin." Three years later Oxford University awarded him with an honorary degree of doctor of law.

By that time, other demands were taking most of Franklin's time. His interest in science and invention, however, never entirely stopped. He invented the odometer, or mileage meter, a device that recorded the turns of a coach or wagon wheel. When his eyesight started to fail, he found himself forced to carry two pairs of glasses, one for reading and eating, the other for distant viewing. Having to constantly change glasses annoyed him. One day an idea popped into his practical mind: Why not combine lenses for close-up and distant viewing in the same frame? He told a lens maker to grind the top part for ordinary use, the bottom part for reading or eating. As with other inventions, Franklin refused to patent bifocal glasses.

Almost forgotten today is Franklin's amazing musical instrument, which he chose to call the armonica. It was nothing at all like the *harmonica* we know today. In fact, the armonica was little like any musical instrument ever invented by anyone else. It had a kind of piano keyboard, except that instead of keys it had thirty-seven glass discs mounted on a bar that spun rapidly around. As the operator kept the discs rotating with a foot treadle, he or she touched the discs to produce the desired notes. Some people called the armonica the sweetest of all instruments, and Mozart and Beethoven wrote special music for it. The instrument surged to popularity in the 1760s, but it proved to be a fad. By 1800 the armonica was largely a museum piece.

Franklin's work on electricity destroys the myth that he was only interested in practical or moneymaking ideas. He devoted most of ten years to electricity. Yet at the time,

Benjamin Franklin's armonica is now on display at the Franklin Institute in Philadelphia.

the lightning rod was the only useful result. Franklin loved knowledge for the sake of knowledge. He thought that his discoveries might have some use in the future. Years later, in 1783, he was to watch the first hot-air balloon in history slowly ascend into the French sky. Someone standing nearby asked him the common questions: What good is it? What use can it ever serve?

Franklin's reply is famous: "Of what use is a new-born baby?"

CHAPTER

9

Citizen Ben Franklin

Benjamin Franklin was a man of many careers. Among other things, he was a writer, a businessman, a scientist, and a public servant. In most cases there are no single dates that stand as milestones to separate the different parts of his life. The careers overlapped in time and blended into one another. His career as a writer, for instance, extended from his teenage years to his death. And he wrote in the interests of business, science, and public service.

All of Franklin's careers came together in the year 1747. He was preparing to turn his printing business over to a partner, David Hall. He was "immersed in electrical experiments." He also found time to write *Plain Truth*. This was a pamphlet intended to wake the citizens of Pennsylvania up to the danger of a French attack.

Waves of trouble with the French had come throughout Franklin's life. Sometimes there would be years of peace. Then war would break out in Europe. As soon as the news reached America, fighting on the frontier would start once again. In the late 1740s, the situation grew worse and worse. Franklin's son, William, in his late teens and yearning for adventure, won an appointment as a junior officer and marched off toward Canada to fight the French.

This time, Benjamin Franklin thought, the fighting might not be confined to the frontier. From the mouth of the Mississippi River, on the south, to the St. Lawrence River, on the north, the French had no access to the sea. It only made sense for the French to try to cut through the middle colonies and win a seaport on the Atlantic Ocean. Where would the French attack? Philadelphia was the most likely place. French boats could sail in from the east to shell the city. At the same time, their troops could attack from the west.

Because of its history, Pennsylvania was ill prepared to meet the French danger. The colony had been founded in 1682 by William Penn, a Quaker. Penn and his associates had received a royal charter making them proprietors of the colony. Now, sixty-five years later, the so-called proprietary lands were controlled by descendants of the original founders. It was their privilege to appoint the governor, and no governor would allow the proprietary lands to be taxed—for any purpose, even necessary defense. Naturally, the rest of the citizens didn't see why they alone should bear the costs of an army. Moreover, one of the Quaker religious beliefs was that war of any kind was evil. The Quakers refused to bear arms, and the proprietors refused to bear taxes.

Franklin's *Plain Truth* may have saved the colony. He

called for a militia, or army of volunteers. Five hundred signed up, then a thousand. To get money, he organized a lottery. There was a widespread call for Franklin to take command of the military force. Saying that he had no experience, he refused. As long as the danger remained, he served his tours of duty as a common soldier.

In 1750, Franklin wrote his mother that when he died, he would rather have people say of him, *"He lived usefully,* than, *He died rich."* His words soon became actions. The next year he was elected to the Pennsylvania Assembly, turning his old job as Assembly clerk over to his son, William. In 1753 he received a royal appointment as deputy postmaster general of North America. The part-time job paid a large salary, 150 pounds a year. Moreover, running a postal service from New England to Virginia would put Franklin in touch with many important people. The same year he was named one of three people to make a treaty with the Ohio Indians at Carlisle, Pennsylvania. After exchanging a round of drinks with the Native Americans, Franklin ordered that the Carlisle taverns serve no more liquor until the treaty was signed. The Native Americans quickly got down to business in a cooperative way.

Because of his success, Franklin was named a delegate to the Albany Congress in 1754. This was a meeting, arranged by the Board of Trade in London, between colonial representatives and the leaders of the Iroquois Confederacy known as the Six Indian Nations. The British government did not want these Native Americans to side with the French in case of future conflict. Except for round after round of speeches, little was accomplished with the Iroquois. The Albany Congress is remembered today because the delegates agreed on what Franklin called his Albany Plan. This was a written proposal that would have allowed the colonies to unite and bear taxation to provide for their own defense. To support the idea, Franklin's *Gazette* published the first political cartoon in American history. Designed and probably drawn by Franklin, it showed a snake cut in eight pieces above the words JOIN, OR DIE.

The Albany Plan was not accepted by any colony. Not one of them was willing to give up even a little of its limited power to decide such matters for itself. Neither was it accepted by the British Crown. In unity there was strength, the London government knew, perhaps strength to be feared. Nevertheless, the Albany Plan did for the first time put the idea of *united states* in the minds of the American people.

Not all of Franklin's time during these years was spent on public duties. At home he still tinkered with electrical equipment. He ran a wire from a lightning rod on the chimney down into his house, where the current divided and passed through two small bells about six inches apart. Between the bells a little brass ball hung from the ceiling by a silk thread. When the bells were electrified, the ball vibrated rapidly between them: RING-G-G-G. One night Franklin was awakened by a loud crack. He left his bed to discover electricity passing from bell to bell "in a continued, dense, white stream, seemingly as large as my finger, whereby the whole staircase was inlightened as with sunshine, so that one might see to pick up a pin."

Debby, however, had little love for the magic bells. For her they rang as an unexpected annoyance. When her husband was away, she found a way to disconnect them. This was probably an excellent idea. Later experts have stated that the bells were a certain way to set fire to the house, sooner or later.

Debby and Ben did share a single love with all their hearts: their daughter, Sally. Little Sally turned eleven in 1754. Franklin considered her "affectionate," "dutiful," "obliging," and "sensible." In short, she had "the best natural disposition in the world." Although William had gone to the best private schools and then studied law, Sally's schooling included little more than basic reading and arithmetic. This was the custom of the time. Her parents were proud of her progress in the "ladylike" arts: needlepoint, music, and dancing. Sally was a happy child and saw no reason to complain.

Away from home, Franklin's duties as postmaster called for trips to all colonies except the Carolinas and Georgia. These were really long, leisurely vacations, lasting several weeks or even months. Franklin traveled in the best style and slept in the best beds. In 1755, however, one of these trips was an urgent one. The British government had tired of depending on local militias and squabbling colonial assemblies to fight the French. Now the Crown had sent General Edward Braddock to America with two full regiments of troops. It was a professional army meant to end the French menace for good. Franklin was to meet Braddock at Frederick, Maryland, on April 22, to arrange the army's postal communications. (This was probably also Franklin's first meeting with a major from Virginia named George Washington.)

Braddock turned out to be a proud man, used to giving orders and completely unused to the colonial way of doing things. He was shocked that he could not simply order all the horses and wagons he wanted. Hundreds would be needed for the campaign against the French. Franklin agreed to help. He hurried to the rich farmland around Lancaster and York, Pennsylvania. There, as he expected, he found the horses, wagons, and drivers. He quickly spent Braddock's eight hundred pounds and another two hundred of his own.

Returning to Braddock's headquarters, Franklin was determined to give the general not only horses and wagons but some advice. He knew that the European style of warfare was no way to fight an army of French soldiers and American Indians on American soil. Not long before, a French force of 1,500 had been destroyed by the Iroquois. Roads were poor, and in many places Braddock's force would have to march single file. Franklin figured that the English army would have to stretch out into a line over four miles long. It could easily be attacked from the side in several places at once. It could be slashed to pieces before the officers could even start to pull things together.

All this meant nothing to the distinguished General Edward Braddock. "These [forces] may, indeed, be a formidable [powerful] enemy to your raw American militia," he told Franklin, "but upon the king's regular and disciplined troops, sir, it is impossible they should make any impression." Braddock was sure he could take Fort Duquesne (near present-day Pittsburgh) in a few days. Then it would be off to Fort Niagara. Weather permitting, Braddock was sure he could seize Quebec in Canada by winter.

Soon Braddock marched off into the fate of Franklin's prediction. Nine miles from Fort Duquesne, the enemy attacked from the woods without warning. A force of about 200 French and Canadians and 600 Native Americans (including fighters from the Potowatomi, the Ottawa, the Delaware, and the Shawnee peoples) defeated a British army of about 1,400 men. Nearly 800 of Braddock's men were killed.

Encouraged by their victory, the French and their

111

Native American allies moved to the east. Soon they were attacking settlements not ninety miles from Philadelphia. Something had to be done—and in a hurry. Franklin used his position in the Assembly to pass a militia bill that provided sixty thousand pounds for defense. This time Franklin himself agreed to take command. With his son, William, at his side, he spent most of the winter of 1755–56 building fortifications and organizing troops for defense. He was hugely popular with the soldiers, who soon gave him the affectionate title "General Franklin."

Still, the basic problem lay with the proprietors. As long as proprietary lands could not be taxed, the colony could not be well defended. William Penn, the first chief proprietor, had been a good man. Although his charter "gave" him Native American lands, he insisted on dealing with the Native Americans in friendship and paying them a decent price. But Penn's two sons, Thomas and Richard, were men of another kind. They had no interest in living in the colonies. Instead, they lived the good life in England on their American rents. They enjoyed all the profits and paid none of the taxes. They also caused constant trouble. For instance, William Penn had once made a treaty with the Delawares. For a fair sum of money, the Delawares gave Penn a piece of land to the west of the Lehigh River. In the quaint language of the time, it was to extend as far as a man could walk in a day and a half. The colonists recognized this as about forty miles. For years the agreement caused no trouble. In 1737, however, Thomas Penn hired expert walkers to cover as much ground as they could in a day and a half. He now claimed 66½ miles. Of course this made the Delawares angry. As late as November 1756, Franklin and others were still negotiating with a group of

Native Americans they knew in their hearts had been cheated.

More and more, it became clear to Pennsylvania leaders that the only sensible negotiations would have to be with the Penns themselves. The proprietors might be under some pressure to accept taxation. If they refused, appeal could be made to both the king and the Parliament (the British legislature). If the English government really knew what was happening, Franklin thought, Pennsylvania might be taken away from the proprietors and placed directly under the Crown as a royal colony. It was decided that Pennsylvania would send an agent to London. There was little argument about who would go—that man of endless charm, wit, patience, knowledge, and experience: Benjamin Franklin.

On June 23, 1757, Franklin sailed for England. Debby, fearing an ocean voyage, stayed behind with Sally. With Franklin went his son, William, to enroll in law school. Father and son each had a slave as a personal servant, called Peter and King, respectively. Franklin was to be paid 1,500 pounds for the trip, and it was expected to take about six months.

Instead, except for one short trip home, Franklin was to stay in England for the next eighteen years. Not until 1775 would he return. Sally would be married. Debby would be in her grave. And a new nation would be about to be born.

CHAPTER

10

The Elder Statesman

Franklin sailed to England on winds of hope. Thirty-three years before, he had arrived in London to find himself stranded, a teenager with little money, no job, and not a friend in the land. Now he made the trip as the official agent of the Pennsylvania Assembly. He had more than enough money. He looked forward to days of good talk with Peter Collinson, with whom he had exchanged letters for years. Another old correspondent was William Strahan. Like Franklin, Strahan was a self-made man, a wealthy printer and publisher. Strahan controlled a respected London newspaper and was himself a member of Parliament, the British lawmaking body.

Franklin also had high hopes for the job he had been given to do. His idea was that all British people, whether they lived in Britain or the American colonies, should consider themselves members of one nation. Back in the colonies, there were already complaints about taxation without representation. Trouble could be avoided, Franklin thought, if the colonists could send representatives to Parliament. After all, why not? The population in the colonies doubled every twenty or twenty-five years. One day the king's subjects in America would outnumber those living in the British Isles. Could the Americans be ruled forever from across the sea? Franklin knew that such a change might take years to accomplish. He had more immediate hopes on the matter of taxing the proprietary estates.

Franklin arrived in London on July 26, 1757. After spending a few days with Peter Collinson, he found a suite of rooms in the comfortable home of a widow named Mrs. Stevenson. The party from Philadelphia soon settled in to their new quarters. William, now a handsome man in his late twenties, entered law school and was soon making friends in high places. Mrs. Margaret Stevenson proved to be not only a landlady but also a good friend. She nursed Benjamin Franklin through a bad illness in November. Ben was especially fond of Mrs. Stevenson's eighteen-year-old daughter, Polly. A most attractive girl, Polly had a quick wit that was almost a match for Franklin's. The two became the best of friends. Franklin became a kind of father to the girl. He gave Polly advice she appreciated. They corresponded for years, long after Polly's marriage and until Franklin's death.

Franklin's official relationships, however, proved to be far from happy. First he paid a call on John Carteret, the earl of Granville, who was president of the Privy Council (something like the president's cabinet in the United States). Franklin had always thought that Pennsylvania laws had to be approved by both the Pennsylvania Assembly and the king. Nonsense, said Granville. The colonial assemblies had only the power the king chose to grant them. At all times, the king's commands were the supreme law in the colonies.

Franklin's meetings with the proprietors, Thomas and Richard Penn, went no better. Their message was the same as Granville's: The Pennsylvania Assembly really had no power. Since Franklin was serving as an agent of that Assembly, he really had no authority either. He did not even have to be recognized. Franklin pointed out that their father, William Penn, had granted the Assembly certain rights in the original charter. The Penns only sneered. William Penn, they told Franklin, had been given no authority by the king to grant such rights. Hence the rights in the original charter did not exist.

Franklin was stunned when he heard the Penns' words. He knew that his face was red and blotchy with anger, but he couldn't help it. The Penns' announcement had come like a sudden declaration of war. On the Penns' faces was "a kind of triumphing, laughing insolence [rudeness]."

Franklin's face was soon redrawn by his inner good nature, but now he knew the job that lay ahead. At first, his victories would have to be small ones. Luckily, he did have a place to start. Peter Collinson and William Strahan were both members of Parliament. They knew people who knew people, all the way up to the king. Also, more and more, Franklin was recognized as an important man in his own right. He was now Dr. Franklin, not only the famous electrical wizard but the author of *The Way to Wealth* and other works. With little effort he could arrange to meet the rich and famous. With a lot of effort, maybe, he could mend the widening crack between Great Britain and its New World colonies.

But it would take longer than six months. Over and over, Ben wrote Debby how much he missed his wife and child, his home and city. Yet over and over, too, the promise of a return home faded into an uncertain future. In 1758 William Strahan, with Franklin's knowledge, wrote a plea to the absent Debby. Ben was an attractive man, Strahan indicated, still of middle years, and London was alive with equally attractive and single ladies. Still, Debby replied that she feared to cross the ocean. Strahan then wrote to David Hall, probably for Debby's hearing: "There are many ladies here that would make no objection to sailing twice as far after him." But again Debby refused.

Ben was probably pretty certain that Debby would stay at home. He knew how she felt. She would be uncomfortable trying to share his new life-style. Ben was now a man of the world. He developed a weekly routine of eating and drinking at different clubs. He made long visits to country estates. In the summertime, when the heat in London almost shut down the government, he took leisurely vacations that lasted up to three months. He visited Scotland, Ireland, the Netherlands, Germany, and France. Celebrities everywhere honored his visits. He wore a powdered wig and dressed in silk. It was an age of gentlemen and ladies, and homsepun Debby just didn't fit the bill.

Some of Franklin's clubs were purely social. Others, like the Junto he had left behind, were devoted to good purposes. One of these was the Associates of Dr. Bray, an organization devoted to the betterment of black people. The anti-slavery movement was more advanced in England than in the colonies. Franklin gained a new respect for black people. He freed Peter—his valet and messenger—sometime during his stay in London.

Unlike Debby, William Franklin had no fear of London society. William was good-looking, smart, charming, and as ambitious as his father. He made his own way through the channels of political power in London. In 1762 he married an aristocratic beauty and was given a prize appointment in the colonies. Late that same year, Ben returned home to attend William's installation as the royal governor of New Jersey. By this time, Ben Franklin had finally won the battle over taxation of the proprietary lands. He intended to stay in Philadelphia for the rest of his life.

The stay lasted exactly two years. What returned him to London was news that the English government was about to pass the Stamp Act. This would be a tax on newspapers, magazines, legal documents, and other kinds of printed matter. Nearly every piece of paper would be illegal unless it bore the required stamps. The stamps could be purchased at special offices run by the British government. To buy the stamp was to pay the tax.

To the Pennsylvania Assembly, the proposed Stamp Act was an outrage. The stamp tax was an internal tax, and therefore illegal. The Assembly declared that it alone could levy taxes within the colony of Pennsylvania. Franklin hurried back to London to protest the tax and to warn what might happen if it became law.

He arrived too late. The hated act was passed by the House of Commons, the lower branch of Parliament, in February 1765 and by the House of Lords, the upper branch, in early March, to go into effect in November. As soon as the news reached America, riots broke out in several cities. Angry mobs paraded through Philadelphia. British offices were attacked. Franklin's enemies—the proprietary party in the Assembly—saw their chance to attack Franklin as well.

For years Franklin's opponents had spread false rumors about him. He was said to be living a life of idleness in London—at public expense. He was said to have jumbled his account books so that he could steal huge sums of money. Now his enemies said that he had lived in England so long that he had, in effect, become an Englishman. Not only had Franklin done nothing to stop the Stamp Act, he had secretly supported it. Hadn't he appointed one of his friends, John Hughes, to be the Stamp Act agent in the colony of Pennsylvania?

In fact, Franklin had only been asked to recommend an agent. He had done so, even though he believed that the act itself was a mistake. But from faraway London, he could do nothing to quiet the violence in the streets. A lawless mob threatened to burn down Franklin's house. Debby and Sally were urged to flee. But Debby stood by her guns— literally. She would stay and defend her husband's honor. When the emergency was over, she reported to Ben in her unique style: "I sente to aske my Brother to Cume and bring his gun all so so we maid one room into a Magazin [magazine, or weapons storehouse]. I ordered sum sorte of defens up Stairs such as I Cold manaig my self." Hundreds of Ben Franklin's supporters had turned out to help Debby Franklin. The mob soon turned to other targets.

The Stamp Act did not go into effect on November 1 as planned, and many people in England urged Parliament to repeal it. Franklin, of course, joined in this effort. He lobbied officials, designed cartoons, and sent a stream of letters off to newspapers. Finally, in February 1766, he got his big chance. Parliament was to reconsider the Stamp Act. Franklin got himself named as one of the experts to appear before the House of Commons. He had never been a good public speaker, so he arranged with friends in Commons to answer their questions. He knew exactly what his friends would ask, and he could easily imagine what the hostile questions would be. He went over the answers beforehand. When the day finally came, he answered over a hundred questions easily, in a calm voice that reflected good sense. His facts and logic carried the day.

A short time later, the Stamp Act was repealed. Franklin had complete copies of his House of Commons appearance printed, with all the questions and all the answers. These were widely distributed in the colonies. Benjamin Franklin was a hero second to none, especially in the city of Philadelphia.

Throughout his years in England, Franklin never lost his sense of humor or his interests in many fields. At the height of the Stamp Act crisis, he wrote a newspaper article making fun of the tall tales that had always circulated in England about the New World. Pretending to be serious, he reported on the "cod and whale fishery" being prepared for the summer season in Canada. Whales love codfish, he wrote, and "when they have a mind to eat cod, pursue them wherever they fly;...the grand leap of the whale in that chase up the fall of Niagara is esteemed, by all who have seen it, as one of the finest spectacles in nature."

Like Ben's wife, Debby, many people of the time had to do their spelling by ear. This was especially true of women, who often received little formal education. When spelling became a problem in the education of Polly Stevenson, Franklin took a serious interest. After all, why shouldn't the symbols used for writing represent the sounds of the spoken language? Franklin analyzed spoken English and produced a phonetic alphabet, or one based on the separate and distinct sounds in the language. To do this, he had to drop some letters and invent new ones. He even had the new alphabet cast in type. But like the International Junto and the Albany Plan, this was to be another great Franklin idea that never caught on.

One of Franklin's favorite vacation spots was the country estate of Bishop Jonathan Shipley at Twyford. Shipley was a good friend. He and his wife had five girls, aged eleven to twenty-three. Franklin and the girls became great friends. As a special treat, Ben asked Debby to send a gray American squirrel, to be given to the Shipley girls as a present. The little animal soon became a household pet. It was called Skugg. Then—as would happen—it was killed by the household dog. Franklin tried to cheer the girls up with an epitaph for Skugg's tiny grave. It is hardly the best of Franklin's writings, but it may be the best known:

> Here Skugg
> Lies snug
> As a bug
> In a rug.

Meanwhile, Franklin continued his diplomatic duties in London. Other colonies besides Pennsylvania had named him as their agent, so that he spoke for more and more people. But the split between Britain and the colonies grew ever wider. For every small success Franklin managed to win, he suffered two setbacks. Still, he kept his hopes alive. He could not believe that Britain would press the colonies to the point of open rebellion. Neither could he believe that the colonies would be foolish enough to revolt against the superior power of England. Any kind of settlement, he thought, would be better than armed conflict. "There never was a good war or a bad peace," he wrote a Boston friend in 1773.

The next year, 1774, brought one disappointment after another. News of the Boston Tea Party reached England in January. To protest a new tax on tea, a group of patriots disguised as Mohawk Indians had boarded three ships in Boston Harbor. Their cargoes of valuable tea were thrown overboard in a rebellious riot. Franklin was not pleased. He knew the protest would only prompt the British to take stern measures. This opinion proved to be right. The Boston Port Bill closed the harbor. In England, Franklin complained to deaf ears. "Where complaining is a crime," he wrote Thomas Cushing of Boston, "hope becomes despair."

Soon after, one of Franklin's letters to Cushing was intercepted by the British and made public. He came close to being tried for treason. Hauled before the Privy Council, he received the verbal whipping of his life. His royal appointment as postmaster was revoked, and with it the salary. Then, from Philadelphia, came news of the first meeting of a Continental Congress. All of Franklin's efforts to keep the peace now seemed a waste of time. Late in the year Debby Franklin suffered a stroke and died. Her sad and disappointed husband made arrangements to sail for home.

On May 5, 1775, Franklin arrived in Philadelphia after a ten-year absence. He made himself comfortable in his old home, now managed by Sally and her husband, Richard Bache. Immediately he was elected to the Continental Congress. Committee work and a long diplomatic mission to Canada kept him busy indeed. A letter to his old London friend William Strahan shows his feelings on the eve of the American Revolution:

Philada July 5, 1775

Mr. Strahan,

You are a member of Parliament, and one of that majority which has doomed my country to destruction. —You have begun to burn our towns, and murder our people. —Look upon your hands! They are stained with the blood of your relations! —You and I were long friends: —You are now my enemy, —and I am

Yours,

B Franklin

In 1776 Franklin was named one of three men to write a statement justifying the creation of a new nation. The Declaration of Independence was actually written by Thomas Jefferson. Franklin made only a few changes, all of them adding bite and force to Jefferson's lofty and somewhat lengthy style. For instance, Jefferson had started the second paragraph, "We hold these truths to be sacred and undeniable,..." Franklin made the words sharper: "We hold these truths to be self-evident,..."

A long struggle lay ahead. The new nation would have to fight for its right to exist. It needed friends—rich friends, powerful friends. France, England's old enemy, seemed to be a logical friend of the new America. Congress decided to send someone to France to negotiate a treaty of friendship and secure aid. But who would that someone be? Benjamin Franklin was seventy now. His health was far from perfect. But he still had that special

Jefferson reads his rough draft of the Declaration of Independence to Franklin in 1776.

charm that made him a good diplomat. Moreover, he had been to France and knew the language.

On October 27, 1776, Franklin sailed for France on the ship *Reprisal*. With him he took two cherished pieces of home—his two grandsons. Benjamin Franklin Bache, Sally's son, was only seven. Franklin adored little Benny, who seemed in a way to replace the long-lost Franky. William Temple Franklin, William's son, was sixteen. There was a special reason for taking William Temple to France. His father, the royal governor of New Jersey, had chosen to remain loyal to England. As a result, the governor had been arrested and sent to a secure American jail in Litchfield, Connecticut. His wife, left alone in New Jersey, was having a hard time of it at best. The boy William Temple would be better off in France.

The crossing was a dangerous one. It was impossible to keep Franklin's trip a secret. If he had been captured at sea by the British, his life would have ended at once. He would have been hanged as a traitor. But the *Reprisal* was an armed ship. Franklin and his grandsons landed safely on French soil on December 3.

Then an amazing thing happened. Franklin found that he was already a very famous man in France. His writings and reputation had preceded him. As he made his way by coach toward Paris, cheering people lined the streets of towns and cities. Franklin was Mr. United States, Mr. Common Man. People strained to catch a glimpse of him, and they loved what they saw. In an age when important men wore powdered wigs, Franklin now chose to wear a huge hat of brown fur. He dressed simply. He even wore his small, metal-framed glasses in public. Glasses were not rare in 1776, but most people thought them an embarrassment. Franklin didn't mind. If glasses helped him to see, he would wear glasses everywhere. It was the honest thing to do, and the French loved him for it.

Soon Franklin was installed in a comfortable house at Passy, a suburb of Paris. He had no idea that his stay in France would be a long one, eight and a half years. During most of the time he was assisted by other American diplomats, John Adams and Thomas Jefferson among them. But Franklin was the only leading American who stayed in France throughout the American Revolution and the long peacemaking process that followed. Franklin was always the leader. He knew the language and the important people. He even won the friendship of King Louis XVI and Queen Marie Antoinette. First he negotiated a treaty of friendship between the United States and France. Then

Benjamin Franklin with his grandsons Benjamin Franklin Bache (right) and William Temple Franklin as they are cheered by Parisians in 1776.

came a steady stream of money and supplies to aid the American cause. In 1778 France formally went to war with England. The American Revolution was really over in 1781, but for Ben Franklin, that only meant that the peace conference in Paris could begin. Not until 1784 were the treaties agreed to by all countries involved.

Important as they were, Franklin's official duties in France took only a small part of his time. He lived the life of a retired gentleman. His cellar at Passy was stocked with hundreds of bottles of the finest French wine. His table was graced with the best cuts of meat. He enjoyed writing playful little poems, essays, and stories. These he printed himself on a small press ordered for his Passy house. Ben Franklin had always enjoyed charming ladies—*charming* both as an adjective and a verb—and he found that many upper-class ladies of France lived for little but their social lives. Debby Franklin would probably have groaned at his endless round of flirtations, innocent as they were.

As the years passed, Franklin himself groaned more and more with physical ailments. Even in middle age he had suffered with gout, a painful swelling of the joints. Now his attacks of gout grew so severe that they sometimes delayed important meetings. To these were added the torment of gallstones. As he neared eighty, Franklin found that he had to move his body carefully. Any sudden jolt made him flinch with pain.

Finally, in May 1785, Franklin received word from the U.S. Congress that his duties in France were over. He could now return home—except that he really couldn't. Even a short ride in a horse-drawn carriage filled his body with agony. A trip to the French coast would be days of torture. Not until July was the problem solved. Queen Marie Antoinette offered Franklin the use of the royal litter. This was a kind of wheelless coach carried between two huge Spanish mules. Franklin found the ride bearable. On July 12, he left Passy, with the mule driver mounted on a third mule and the two grandsons following in a carriage with a good French friend. The party began its slow trip to the Atlantic coast. Six days later they reached the port of Havre.

On September 14, Franklin's ship tied up at a Philadelphia dock. The crowd cheered. Bells chimed. Cannons roared. After the hero's welcome, Franklin again moved in with his daughter's family. But now there were six Bache children, and his house was crowded. An addition to the house soon gave Franklin the comfort he wanted.

Franklin had returned from his years in England in time to help with the Declaration of Independence. Now he returned from France in time for the Constitutional Convention. The convention was held in the hot summer of 1787 in Philadelphia, in a building near Franklin's house. Franklin was an old man now. Nobody really minded when his eyes closed slowly as he nodded off to sleep in his chair. The records show that Franklin said little during the long convention. But the records also show that he suggested the "Great Compromise" that made the Constitution possible. The states with big populations—Massachusetts, Pennsylvania, and Virginia—wanted representation in Congress to be based on population. After all, states with more people should have a larger voice. The states with fewer people, of course, wanted each state to have the same number of representatives in Congress. Franklin proposed that there be two houses of Congress. A Senate would give each state two votes. A House of Representatives would give each state the power of its population—that is, representation in proportion to the number of people. Bills would have to pass both houses before they became law.

On the final day of the long convention, Franklin urged all the delegates to sign the Constitution—even if they, like Benjamin Franklin himself, disliked some parts of the document. As the last signers added their names, Franklin turned to a few delegates near him. He pointed at George Washington's chair. Washington, the president of the convention, had always sat in a large chair with a sun painted on its back. For weeks, Franklin said, he had looked at that sun behind Washington "without being able to tell whether it was rising or setting. But now at length I have the happiness to know that it is a rising and not a setting sun."

Franklin was right. A new nation called the United States of America was on the rise. But as the sun of the new nation climbed proudly into the sky, Franklin's own sun was setting. He was to live for three more years, slowly losing both strength and energy. Even at the end of his life, however, Franklin managed to keep working. He went on writing his autobiography. He became president of the Pennsylvania Society for Promoting the Abolition of Slavery. Officials in the North as well as the South received Franklin's pleas, since slave ships from his native New England were still doing a brisk business on the Atlantic. The first antislavery petition ever received by the Congress of the United States came from Benjamin Franklin.

In the spring of 1790, Franklin again fell victim to pleurisy, the illness that had twice nearly ended his life. This time he felt sure that the disease would win the battle. One day, feeling himself near death, he got out of his bed and asked Sally to make it up neatly. Ben Franklin had

Charles Wilson Peale painted this portrait of Benjamin Franklin in 1789, the year before Franklin's death.

always been a clean and tidy man. He told his daughter that he didn't want to die in a messy bed.

Not long after, on the evening of April 17, Benjamin Franklin died peacefully. His death was mourned in every city and town. The whole nation rose to honor the life of a native son whose glory would never fade.

Important Dates

1706 Benjamin Franklin is born in Boston, Massachusetts, on January 17, the son of Josiah and Abiah Franklin.

1714–16 Franklin attends elementary school for two years, the total of his formal education.

1718 Franklin is apprenticed to his brother James, a printer.

1722 Writing as "Silence Dogood," Franklin has fourteen essays printed in *The New England Courant.*

1723 Increasing trouble with his brother James prompts Franklin to leave Boston in secret. In Philadelphia he finds work with printer Samuel Keimer.

1724–26 Unkept promises of Governor William Keith of Pennsylvania leave Franklin stranded in London. He works as a printer for a year and a half before returning home.

1727 Franklin founds his famous Junto, a club to further the education and business success of ambitious young men.

1728 Franklin sets himself up in the printing business, at first with partner Hugh Meredith.

1729 Franklin begins publishing *The Pennsylvania Gazette,* soon to be the most popular newspaper in America.

1730 Franklin enters into a common-law marriage with Deborah (Read) Rogers.

1732 The 1733 issue of *Poor Richard's Almanack* is published. Franklin continues the popular almanac for twenty-five years.

1744 After three years of experimenting, Franklin publishes a long pamphlet on his *New Invented Pennsylvanian Fireplaces.*

1748 Franklin retires from active life as a printer, intending to devote the rest of his years to scientific research and good works.

1751 The first edition of Franklin's *Experiments and Observations on Electricity* is published in London. Franklin is elected to the Pennsylvania Assembly.

1752 With his son, William, Franklin conducts his famous kite experiment.

1754 Franklin proposes his Albany Plan, an unsuccessful attempt to unite the American colonies for purposes of defense.

1755–56 After the defeat of British General Edward Braddock near present-day Pittsburgh, Franklin organizes and commands a citizens' army to defend the region against the French and their Native American allies.

1757–75 Except for two years, Franklin serves as a colonial agent in London. His efforts fail to prevent the coming revolution in the colonies.

1762 Franklin describes his amazing musical instrument, the *armonica,* in a letter to a friend. The invention proved to be a popular fad.

1776 Franklin assists Thomas Jefferson in writing the Declaration of Independence. Late in the year he leaves for France, to spend the war years representing American interests in Paris.

1784 Franklin invents bifocal glasses, commenting that they help him "hear" better because he can now see both the food on his plate and the mouths of others at the table who are speaking French.

1785 With the peace treaty finally signed and ratified, Franklin returns to Philadelphia.

1787 At the age of eighty-one, Franklin attends the Constitutional Convention and makes important contributions.

1790 Benjamin Franklin dies in his Philadelphia home on the night of April 17.

Bibliography

Aldridge, Alfred Owen. *Benjamin Franklin: Philosopher and Man.* Philadelphia and New York: J. B. Lippincott Co., 1965.

Bowen, Catherine Drinker. *The Most Dangerous Man in America: Scenes from the Life of Benjamin Franklin.* Boston and Toronto: Little, Brown and Co., 1974.

*Donovan, Frank R. *The Many Worlds of Benjamin Franklin.* New York: American Heritage Publishing Co./Harper & Row, 1963.

Franklin, Benjamin. *The Autobiography of Benjamin Franklin and Selections from His Writings.* New York: Random House, Inc., 1944. Available in many editions, hardcover and paperback.

Franklin, Benjamin. *Benjamin Franklin: A Biography in His Own Words.* Edited by Thomas Fleming. New York: Newsweek/Harper & Row, 1972.

Franklin, Benjamin. *Benjamin Franklin: Writings.* New York: Library of America/Viking Press, 1987.

Franklin, Benjamin. *The Papers of Benjamin Franklin.* 27 vols. Edited by Leonard W. Labaree and others. New Haven, Conn.: Yale University Press, 1959–1988.

Franklin, Benjamin. *The Works of Benjamin Franklin.* 12 vols. Edited by John Bigelow. New York: G. P. Putnam's Sons, 1904.

*Meltzer, Milton. *Benjamin Franklin: The New American.* New York, Toronto, London, and Sydney: Franklin Watts, 1988.

Wright, Esmond. *Franklin of Philadelphia.* Cambridge, Mass.: Belknap/Harvard University Press, 1986.

Van Doren, Carl. *Benjamin Franklin.* New York: The Viking Press, 1938.

*Readers of the Pioneers in Change book *Benjamin Franklin* may find this book particularly readable.

Index

Addison, Joseph, 18–19
African Americans, 2, 21, 80, 113, 117–118, 129
Albany Congress, 108–109
Albany Plan, 108–109, 121, 132
alcoholism, 46–47, 59, 70, 75
American Indians. *See* Native Americans
American Philosophical Society, 93
American Revolution, 123, 125–127
American Weekly Mercury (newspaper), 73
armonica, 104, 105, 132
Associates of Dr. Bray, 117–118

Bache, Benjamin Franklin (grandson), 125, 126, 128
Bache, Richard (son-in-law), 122
Bache, Sarah ("Sally") Franklin (daughter), 90, 110, 113, 119, 122, 125, 128, 129
bifocal glasses, 1, 104, 125–126, 134
Boston, 2–3, 16, 21, 22, 26, 28, 30, 31, 34, 35, 38, 41, 42, 43–44, 46, 73, 81, 95
Boston Tea Party, 122
Braddock, Edward, 110–111, 132
Bradford, Andrew, 31, 39, 40, 73, 74, 83
Bradford, William, 31

Canada and Canadians, 111
Carteret, John (earl of Granville), 115–116
Coleman, William, 75
Collins, James, 18, 28, 45, 46–48, 62, 89
Collinson, Peter, 95–96, 100, 103, 114, 115, 116
Connecticut, 30
Constitution (U.S.), 1, 95, 128–129
Constitutional Convention, 128–129, 133

Cushing, Thomas, 122

Declaration of Independence, 1, 95, 123, 124, 132
Delaware, 41, 53, 74
Denham, Thomas, 55, 60, 65

electricity, 1, 95–104, 104–105, 106, 109
England, 2, 3–4, 12, 64, 89, 90, 96, 108–109, 110–111, 112, 114–122, 125, 127. *See also* London
Essays to Do Good (Mather), 18, 25

France and the French, 3, 31, 96, 100, 106–108, 110–111, 117, 123, 125–127
Franklin, Abiah Folger (mother), 4, 5, 10, 44, 45, 108
Franklin, Anne, 4
Franklin, Benjamin
  armonica, 104, 105
  Albany Plan, 108–109, 132
  bifocal glasses, 1, 104, 132
  birth, 2, 131
  as a businessman, 63, 70, 72–73, 74, 75, 79, 80, 81, 82, 90, 91, 106, 131
  candle and soap making, 7–9
  character, 2, 6, 8, 11, 16, 18–20, 30, 41, 44, 45–46, 55, 56–57, 58, 62–63, 68, 70, 72, 80, 87, 88–89
  chronology of important dates, 131–133
  clerk of the Pennsylvania Assembly, 90, 91, 108
  colonial agent in London, 113, 114–118
  Constitution (U.S.), 1, 128–129
  death, 130, 133

About the Author

Robert R. Potter, educator and author, has taught on levels from junior high to graduate school and written seventeen books including *Buckminster Fuller,* another biography in the Pioneers in Change series. Potter received his Ed.D. in English education from Columbia University. He is the author of *Making Sense* (Globe Book Company), an acclaimed introduction to general semantics for secondary school students. Potter now lives with his family in West Cornwall, Connecticut, where he has served on school boards for fifteen years. He is a member of the National Council of Teachers of English, the Institute of General Semantics, and the Maple Syrup Producers Association of Connecticut.